HOME OFFICE

THE HILLSBOROUGH STADIUM DISASTER

15 APRIL 1989

INQUIRY BY
THE RT HON LORD JUSTICE TAYLOR

FINAL REPORT

*Presented to Parliament
by the Secretary of State for the Home Department
by Command of Her Majesty
January 1990*

First Published 1990
Reprinted 1998
£12.60

Cm 962

CONTENTS

PART IV – THE FOOTBALL SPECTATORS ACT 1989

Photographs are reproduced by courtesy of:–

Ballast Nedam   (Appendices 5 and 7)
Mr Norman Bush   (Appendix 6)
BBT Gargini   (Appendix 8)

The Rt Hon David Waddington QC, MP
Secretary of State for the Home Department

THE HILLSBOROUGH STADIUM DISASTER
15 APRIL 1989

FINAL REPORT OF INQUIRY

INTRODUCTION

1. On 17 April 1989 I was appointed by your predecessor, the Rt Hon Douglas Hurd CBE, MP to carry out an Inquiry with the following terms of reference:

"To inquire into the events at Sheffield Wednesday Football Ground on 15 April 1989 and to make recommendations about the needs of crowd control and safety at sports events."

2. Two Assessors were appointed to assist me: Mr Brian Johnson CBE, QPM, DL, Chief Constable of Lancashire, and Professor Leonard Maunder OBE, BSc, PhD, ScD, FEng, FI Mech E, Professor of Mechanical Engineering at the University of Newcastle upon Tyne.

3. The first stage of the Inquiry was primarily concerned with the investigation of events at Hillsborough Stadium on 15 April 1989 when 95 people were crushed to death at a Cup semi-final match between Liverpool and Nottingham Forest.

4. Over 31 days between 15 May and 29 June, I heard oral evidence from 174 witnesses at a public hearing in Sheffield. I also received much written evidence by way of submissions and letters.

5. On 1 August 1989 I presented an Interim Report setting out my findings as to how and why the disaster occurred. Also, in accordance with your predecessor's wishes, I made interim recommendations aimed at preventing any further disaster and improving safety in the short term.

6. The Interim Report and its recommendations had of necessity to be made quickly so that action could be taken before the start of the new football season due to open in mid August. Despite all the speed I could muster, the recommendations left very little time for pre-season action, especially in Scotland where the fixture list started earlier than in England and Wales. I must pay tribute to the clubs, local authorities, police and other services for responding so promptly and for implementing the recommendations so wholeheartedly.

7. In my Interim Report I indicated that it would be necessary to conduct wider and deeper investigations before delivering a Final Report on the needs of crowd control and safety for the future. Accordingly, I invited and have considered a large number of written submissions describing present practices and problems and suggesting future changes. Those who have contributed are listed at Appendix 1. I am extremely grateful to all of them for their time and their views. I expect there are a number of contributors and correspondents who may look in vain for comment on each and every point they have raised. I hope they will understand that time and space make it necessary to be selective and to have regard to the main issues.

8. I have also had numerous informal meetings with those representing relevant public bodies, clubs and spectator interests. These have been conducted as private discussion sessions rather than hearings of oral evidence thereby enabling controversial issues to be explored and theories tested.

9. In all of this I have continued to be assisted by the two Assessors. Each holds a professional appointment carrying heavy responsibility and I am deeply grateful to both for devoting so much time to assisting me. Their contributions have been of the highest value. While the sole responsibility for this report is mine, I am comforted in the knowledge that both Assessors agree with it.

10. At my request, Professor Maunder chaired a Technical Working Party to review the technical aspects of the Home Office Guide to Safety at Sports Grounds (1986 edition), "The Green Guide". Each member of his team has much relevant experience and the team was well qualified for its task. I am most grateful for the co-operation and efforts of each member. The Report of the Technical Working Party is at Appendix 3.

11. In the course of the Inquiry, the two Assessors and I have between us visited 31 sports grounds. They are listed at Appendix 2. Of those, 24 were soccer grounds, but we also attended at grounds featuring Rugby Union, Rugby League, cricket, tennis and golf. I wish to record our thanks to the club officials who so readily

and hospitably facilitated our visits; also to the officers of local government, the police and the emergency services who together with club officials conducted us round the grounds, explained their operations and answered our questions fully and frankly. Seeing crowd control and behaviour before, during and after a match from various sections of the viewing areas was an essential source of first hand knowledge. It brought alive the written and oral reports we received.

12. I should like to express my thanks to the Home Office team who have staffed this Inquiry so well. Mr Robert Whalley was appointed as its Secretary. He has handled all the administrative arrangements impeccably and has given much invaluable advice and assistance on every aspect of the Inquiry. He was ably and diligently assisted by Mr Jonathan Sweet, Mrs Margaret Wither, Mr Tony Moore, Mrs Kate Humphries from the Home Office and my own Clerk Mr Ernest Pott. I also renew my thanks to the West Midlands Police, and, in particular, to Mr Geoffrey Dear QPM, DL, LLB, the Chief Constable, and Mr Mervyn Jones MSc, Assistant Chief Constable in full-time charge of the investigation, who have continued to provide me with helpful information at this second stage of the Inquiry.

13. Having made my findings as to the events at Hillsborough, I do not in this report say any more about them save by way of illustration. I am aware that inquests are still to be held, civil proceedings are in motion and the possibility of criminal charges is under consideration. However, those are not matters for me. I therefore turn now to broader issues as promised in paragraph 304 of my Interim Report.

14. My terms of reference are extremely wide. They embrace crowd control and safety at sports events of all kinds. However, crowd problems are directly related to the nature of the event and the numbers attending it. Realistically, this means that attention needs to be concentrated on events within the scope of the Safety of Sports Ground Act 1975 and the Fire Safety and Safety of Places of Sport Act 1987. Even more specifically, the emphasis in this Report is especially upon football. The Hillsborough disaster and indeed other disasters before it occurred in crowded football stadia. The numbers and the atmosphere at a football match have created special problems such as overcrowding and misbehaviour not, so far, to be found to a like degree elsewhere.

15. That football is a special case has been expressly recognised by the Government in promoting the Football Spectators Act 1989. The Bill received the Royal Assent on 16 November 1989. It had commenced its course through Parliament before the Hillsborough disaster. Expressly because of that disaster and the setting up of this Inquiry it reached the statute book under unusual conditions. It was always to be an enabling Act whose implementation would require a Statutory Instrument. In order to have the provisions of the Act in place as soon as possible, the Government decided to proceed with it forthwith, notwithstanding Hillsborough and this Inquiry. That decision was subject to an undertaking to bring the matter back before Parliament on two separate occasions. First, before the appointment of the Football Membership Authority under the Act; secondly, to debate the scheme which the Act provides should be drawn up by that Authority.

16. I was expressly told by your predecessor upon my appointment that my terms of reference included consideration of the national membership scheme provided for in the Bill. That was confirmed on numerous occasions by Ministers in the course of the Bill's passage through Parliament. It was made clear that although the Act would be on the statute book before my Final Report, Parliament would have the opportunity to consider any observations I might make, including any about the national membership scheme. Thus, to take only two examples, Mr Nicholas Ridley, then Secretary of State for the Environment, said on the Second Reading of the Bill on 27 June 1989:

"I began by referring to Lord Justice Taylor's inquiry. I will emphasise again now what I said at the beginning. Parliament will have not one but two opportunities to debate and vote on the national membership scheme after we have received the report and in the light of any comments that Justice Taylor may make on the scheme. By proceeding with the Bill now, we can put the framework for the scheme in place and make it possible to move on rapidly with the scheme, if Parliament agrees that we should do so when it has seen what Lord Justice Taylor has to say."
(Official Report, column 850).

Secondly, at the Committee stage on 6 July 1989, Mr Colin Moynihan, the Minister for Sport, said:

"I am certain that Lord Justice Taylor will feel in no way inhibited by consideration of the Bill in our suggested format, because we specifically amended the Bill to provide for the Secretary of State's approval of the scheme after the final report. .... the Bill is amended to enable the House to consider in detail the recommendations before we establish the Football Membership Authority to draw up the scheme. ....To hypothesise on whether Lord Justice Taylor is in favour of a national membership scheme or whether he

may not even comment on it, is totally irrelevant because the Bill provides for the House of Commons and House of Lords to consider the report before setting up a Football Membership Authority."
(Official Report, column 56).

17. It must be a rare if not unique situation for a judge, appointed to conduct an Inquiry, to have within his remit consideration of the merits and provisions of an Act of Parliament already in place. It cannot be for a judge to opine upon the wisdom or terms of an Act expressing the established will of Parliament. But, where Parliament has passed an Act in such terms and upon such undertakings as expressly to provide that the Inquiry judge be uninhibited in commenting upon it and that Parliament should have the opportunity to consider his comments in further debate, then I conceive it to be his duty to express his views. My doing so should not be interpreted as showing any lack of the respect and deference due to Parliament. Not to do so, against the background I have described, would surely be thought surprising if not pusillanimous.

18. In Part I of this Report I state some lessons to be learnt from Hillsborough, examine the state of football today and propose a range of measures to give it a better future. In Part II I consider, in detail, measures to improve safety at sports grounds. Part III is concerned with crowd control at sports grounds and various strategies for dealing with hooligans. In Part IV I consider the provisions of the 1989 Act regarding the national membership scheme. Finally, at the end of the text, I set out my Recommendations. So as to avoid confusion, I have not set out my Interim Recommendations for the purpose of comparison. Hardly any excisions have been made. Where I have decided to repeat or amend the Interim Recommendations, they are included in the single list of Final Recommendations. I hope this Report and the Final Recommendations may be instrumental in promoting better and safer conditions at sports grounds in the future.

18 January 1990   PETER TAYLOR

PART I – FOOTBALL: PRESENT AND FUTURE

CHAPTER 1

THREE SOMBRE LESSONS AFTER HILLSBOROUGH

i. Previous Reports Unheeded

19.   It is a depressing and chastening fact that mine is the ninth official report covering crowd safety and control at football grounds. After eight previous reports and three editions of the Green Guide, it seems astounding that 95 people could die from overcrowding before the very eyes of those controlling the event. In January 1986, Mr Justice Popplewell, whose report following the Bradford Disaster was the eighth in the series, summarised those of his seven predecessors. The Shortt Report of 1924 followed disorder at the Cup Final of 1923. The Moelwyn Hughes Report of 1946 followed the disaster at Bolton Wanderers ground when overcrowding caused 33 deaths. In 1966 the Government commissioned the Chester Report on "The State of Association Football". The Harrington Report of 1968 drew attention to problems of crowd behaviour and led to the Lang Report of 1969 on the same subject. In 1972, Lord Wheatley's Report on Crowd Safety at Sports Grounds followed the disaster at Ibrox Park where 66 spectators died. The McElhone Report of 1977 on Football Crowd Behaviour of Scottish supporters was commissioned by the Secretary of State for Scotland. In 1984 an Official Working Group on Football Spectator Violence set up by the Department of Environment presented a further report.

20.   As a result of the Wheatley Report, the first edition of the Green Guide was issued in 1973, and Parliament passed the Safety of Sports Grounds Act 1975. A second edition of the Green Guide was issued in 1976 and a third edition in 1986 incorporated recommendations made by Mr Justice Popplewell.

21.   Introducing his excellent and concise summary of the previous reports, Mr Justice Popplewell said:

"almost all the matters into which I have been asked to inquire and almost all the solutions I have proposed, have been previously considered in detail by many distinguished Inquiries over a period of 60 years".

Because his citations from those earlier reports are still highly relevant, I append his summary of them at Appendix 4.

22.   In my Interim Report I set out what happened at Hillsborough and why. That it was allowed to happen, despite all the accumulated wisdom of so many previous reports and guidelines must indicate that the lessons of past disasters and the recommendations following them had not been taken sufficiently to heart. I appreciate how easy it is to criticise with hindsight and that a new situation can always arise in human affairs which has not previously been envisaged. But many of the deficiencies at Hillsborough *had* been envisaged.

23.   The Moelwyn Hughes Report in 1924 had stressed the need to start controlling the crowd well back from the entrance to the ground. The Green Guide required that "Turnstiles should be of such numbers as to admit spectators at a rate whereby no unduly large crowds are kept waiting for admission" (paragraph 44). Chapter 8 of the Guide required "Arrangements should be made ... to contain pressures before they reach dangerous proportions". Chapter 16 laid down maximum capacity which was grossly exceeded in the fatal pens at Hillsborough. Both the Green Guide (Chapter 15) and Mr Justice Popplewell had stated the need for gates in the perimeter fencing to be adequate to permit escape on to the pitch in an emergency. Why were these recommendations and others not followed? I suggest two main reasons. First, insufficient concern and vigilance for the safety and well-being of spectators. This was compounded by a preoccupation with measures to control hooliganism. Secondly, complacency which led all parties to think that since disaster had not occurred on previous occasions it would not happen this time. But there is no point in holding inquiries or publishing guidance unless the recommendations are followed diligently. That must be the first lesson.

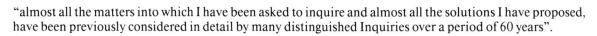

ii. "It Couldn't Happen Here"

24.   Amazingly, complacency was still to be found even after Hillsborough. It was chilling to hear the same refrain from directors at several clubs I visited:–

"Hillsborough was horrible – but, of course, it couldn't have happened here."

Couldn't it? The Hillsborough ground was regarded by many as one of the best in the country. It was selected

4

by the FA for the Cup semi-final and thought by them to be entirely suitable. The identical fixture had passed off uneventfully the previous year. I have little doubt that if the disaster scenario had been described to the management at Hillsborough prior to 15 April, they too would have said "Of course, it couldn't happen here". Yet something like it had happened at Hillsborough in 1981, albeit with less dire results. Moreover, I am satisfied from eyewitness accounts I have received that there have been many other occasions when overcrowding has led, at various grounds round the country, to a genuine apprehension of impending disaster through crushing, averted only by good fortune. I have heard from Police Commanders at a number of the grounds I have visited how relieved they are that capacities have been reduced in the interests of safety.

25. So, although the operational errors on 15 April were special to one ground and one day, the lack of precautions against overcrowding was not unique. I do not believe that sufficient safety measures were being applied at all other grounds. The lesson here is that Hillsborough should not be regarded as a freak occurrence, incapable of happening elsewhere. All those responsible for certifying, using and supervising sports grounds should take a hard look at their arrangements and keep doing so. Complacency is the enemy of safety.

iii. A Blight on Football

26. Football is our national game. We gave it to the world. But its image in our country has been much tarnished. In my Interim Report I concentrated on overcrowding because it was the cause of the Hillsborough disaster. But wider and deeper inquiry shows that overcrowding is only one feature amongst a number causing danger or marring football as a spectator sport. The picture revealed is of a general malaise or blight over the game due to a number of factors. Principally these are: old grounds, poor facilities, hooliganism, excessive drinking and poor leadership. Crowd safety and crowd behaviour with which I am concerned are closely related to the quality of the accommodation and facilities offered and to the standards which are encouraged and enforced. So I think it necessary to consider all these aspects.

Old Grounds

27. Because we were first into the field, most of our football grounds are now elderly. Between 1889 and 1910, 58 of the clubs belonging to the current League moved into the grounds they now occupy.* Many of them are ill-placed on cramped sites boxed into residential areas. When they were built, they were not intended to cater for the stream of coaches, vans and cars which now arrive and require parking space. Inside the grounds decay and dilapidation are often extensive. The terrace accommodation, in particular, is often uncovered and little has been done to improve the layout in accordance with modern expectations. This is chiefly because the safety and comfort of those on the terraces has not been regarded as a priority. In fairness, limitations of space at some grounds make it very difficult to achieve a layout appropriate to present day needs. By contrast, clubs in Europe and South America have the advantage of grounds built more recently on more spacious sites and planned to meet modern conditions. Where improvements have been made to our grounds they have often been patchy and piecemeal. This approach is itself a threat to safety. To build a seated stand over a standing area, to enlarge or divide a terrace, to rearrange exits and entrances or to modify turnstile areas - any of these measures is fraught with safety implications. Yet often such changes have been made to achieve one purpose without sufficient thought about the adverse side-effects which could result.

28. This was exemplified by the sequence of alterations at the Leppings Lane end at Hillsborough. Radial fences were installed to divide up the terraces; this led to a reduction in the system of crush barriers. The area inside the turnstiles was altered for purposes of segregation. Old signs were not removed; new signs were inadequate. The result was a bewildering complex which contributed to the delivery of excessive numbers down the tunnel into pens 3 and 4.

Poor Facilities

29. Football spectators are invited by the clubs for entertainment and enjoyment. Often, however, the facilities provided for them have been lamentable. Apart from the discomfort of standing on a terrace exposed to the elements, the ordinary provisions to be expected at a place of entertainment are sometimes not merely basic but squalid. At some grounds the lavatories are primitive in design, poorly maintained and inadequate in number. This not only denies the spectator an essential facility he is entitled to expect. It directly lowers standards of conduct. The practice of urinating against walls or even on the terraces has become endemic and is followed by men who would not behave that way elsewhere. The police, who would charge a man for urinating in the street, either tolerate it in football grounds or do no more than give a verbal rebuke. Thus crowd conduct becomes degraded and other misbehaviour seems less out of place.

30. The refreshments available to supporters are often limited and of indifferent quality. They are sold in

*Inglis: Football Grounds of Great Britain p 10

5

surrounding streets from mobile carts and inside many grounds from other carts or from shoddy sheds. Fans eat their hamburgers or chips standing outside in all weathers. There is a prevailing stench of stewed onions. Adequate numbers of bins for rubbish are often not available; so wrappings, containers and detritus are simply dropped. This inhospitable scene tends to breed bad manners and poor behaviour. The atmosphere does not encourage pride in the ground or consideration for others. I accept that many fans are quite content to eat on the hoof when visiting a match, but there is no reason why the fare available should not be wholesome, varied and decently served from clean and attractive outlets. Fast food establishments meeting these requirements are readily to be found at railway stations and on high streets; why not at football grounds?

31. At most grounds little attempt has been made to provide pre-match entertainment. To do so could have a double advantage. It would give the spectators more value for their money. It could also bring them in earlier thereby avoiding congestion at the turnstiles in the last few minutes before kick-off. Such entertainment as has been tried has mostly failed to appeal to the spectators. They do not seem drawn by the musical offerings of the disc jockey or by marching bands. The football supporters' organisations complain that supporters have not hitherto been much consulted about this or about anything else affecting their well-being and enjoyment.

32. In giving this dismal account of the football scene, I have taken care to use the words "often", "at most grounds" or "at many grounds". I acknowledge that there are notable exceptions where great improvements have been effected and I do not suggest that every disagreeable feature I have described is to be found at every ground. Nevertheless, the overall picture of conditions and facilities to be expected by a standing spectator is depressing. It is in stark contrast to the different world, only yards away, in the Board Room and the lucrative executive boxes. I appreciate that they cater for an affluent clientele and bring in much-needed revenue. No one would expect or indeed want their plush carpeting or haute cuisine when visiting the terraces; but accommodation and facilities have often been below the basic decent standard necessary to give spectators dignity let alone comfort.

33. It is small wonder that attendances at matches gradually fell off from a peak of 77 million in the season 1949/50 to about 20 million in the late 1980s. No doubt other reasons played their part; for example, the emergence of other spectator sports and television. Until the 1960s most men worked on a Saturday morning and many went straight to the match in the afternoon. But the 5 day week together with increased car ownership made Saturday outings for the family a popular activity. On top of these factors, however, the prospect of attending football in the conditions I have described clearly became unattractive to many erstwhile supporters. Added to this was the fear of disorder. So far, I have not mentioned the further indignities endured by supporters as a result of hooliganism and the measures taken to contain it.

Hooliganism

34. During the 1970s, hooligan behaviour became a scourge at and around football grounds. Rival fans abused and fought with each other on the terraces. The pitch was invaded, sometimes to facilitate the fighting, sometimes in an attempt to abort a match by those whose team was losing and on occasions to display anger and seek to assault a referee or a player who had incurred displeasure. Throwing missiles, either at a player or a policeman or at rival fans, became another violent feature. When the police responded by searching fans for missiles on entry, the practice grew of throwing coins (which could not be confiscated). Sometimes the coins were sharpened in advance to make them more damaging.

35. Mass singing of traditional songs, some of nation-wide appeal, some local to the area or the club, had become a part of the terrace culture. But the repertoire became augmented and degraded by abusive and obscene chants aimed at the referee or the opposing fans. A further nasty addition was racist chanting aimed at any black player of either team.

36. Hooliganism outside the ground also became rife. Supporters of rival teams abused and attacked each other. Hooligan gangs caused damage to trains, to buses, and to property on their route. Some deliberately went out of their way to rampage through local shops, stealing, wrecking and intimidating as they went - an activity known as "steaming". After a match, rival supporters would attack each other on the way home in the street, in public transport or in public houses.

Segregation

37. To contain and control these manifold forms of anti-social and criminal behaviour there is now an elaborate complex of measures. The policy of segregation was born in the 1970s. Gradually, it has called for more and more extreme and expensive strategies by the clubs and the police. As each measure taken has been circumvented by determined hooligans, further measures have had to be grafted on to the system. Witnessing the full florid exercise taking place every Saturday afternoon nowadays makes one wonder how anyone could have contemplated going to such lengths to facilitate the watching of football. But nobody did; it just grew.

38. Clubs have sub-divided their grounds to keep rival fans apart by putting fencing and sterile areas between them, by screening them from inciting each other, by separate entrances and exits and by perimeter fences round the pitch. Many of the fences are very high and are crowned with elaborate spikes and barbed wire, the top sections being inclined inwards to prevent their being scaled. At some grounds a telescopic tunnel is extended on to the pitch to protect the teams from missiles as they come on or go off.

39. The police start and finish their segregation exercise well away from the ground. Typically, special trains or coaches carrying the away supporters are monitored en route. The police meet them and escort the fans with mounted officers, dog handlers and foot officers, ensuring they go only to their allotted section of the ground. They are searched at the entrance for drink or weapons (as are the home fans). They are then confined in an area caged by fencing for the duration of the match. When it ends, the away supporters are often held back for a quarter to half an hour whilst the home supporters are dispersed. They are then escorted away in the same manner as they arrived and put back on to their trains or buses. Although the main body of away supporters can thus be policed as a group, those who arrive independently in cars or vans have freedom of manoeuvre. Occasionally trouble makers get into the wrong area and a violent episode occurs. Again, the further away from the ground the spectators spread, the less the police can do to prevent sporadic confrontations. By and large however, the police measures have worked to prevent violent outbursts in and around the ground.

40. But at what a price! In addition to the poor facilities I described earlier (which are often worse for away than for home fans) the ordinary law-abiding football supporter travelling away is caught up in a police operation reminiscent of a column of prisoners of war being marched and detained under guard. I watched the escort of Arsenal fans after a match at Stamford Bridge. They were held in the ground for thirty-five minutes while the Chelsea supporters left. They were then escorted by a substantial body of police to Fulham Broadway underground station. There, to avoid overcrowding on the platform, they were admitted to the station only in measured groups. Special trains were run to take them non-stop into the centre of the city to avoid clashes at nearby stations.

41. Clearly, the police with their great experience of controlling crowds at the ground considered this strategy was necessary in the present climate. Their views were confirmed in that despite their efficient and good humoured management of the match and its aftermath, scuffles took place when some fans got into the wrong section of the ground. Moreover such police practice is not unique to our country. There are similar hooligan problems for example in Holland. I witnessed a very similar operation carried out by the Dutch police at Utrecht to control a train load of supporters from Eindhoven.

42. Necessary though such operations may presently be, they do nothing to enhance the image of football as a spectator sport followed for entertainment and pleasure. I know of no other sport or entertainment in a civilised country in which it is necessary to keep those attending from attacking each other.

43. Apart from their impact on the spectator, operations to control football crowds have other serious repercussions. The cost in money, manpower and disruption is enormous. Last year, the cost of policing football in London was some £10 million of which only £1 million could be recovered from the clubs. According to the Football Trust, who meet one third of the costs of police charges incurred by clubs at matches for the Football League, Scottish Football League and GM Vauxhall Conference, the cost to clubs during 1988/89 was £4.79 million. Since this relates only to costs inside grounds which can be recovered by the police, the total cost to the police service is substantially more. Her Majesty's Chief Inspector of Constabulary for England and Wales said, in his annual report for 1988, that:-

"Football continues to be a focus for hooliganism ... demands on the police service continued at a high level. Typically, 5000 officers may be engaged on football duties on Saturdays during the football season."

The Home Office estimate that the total cost of deploying these officers is perhaps £200,000 to £300,000 each football Saturday. At many League matches, policing requires some 300 officers in the ground with many more outside and others performing related traffic duties. At high risk matches, Cup semi-finals and the like, even greater numbers are deployed. At Hillsborough there were 800 officers in and around the ground. Obviously officers deployed to football cannot be performing police duties elsewhere. Although many are brought in on an overtime basis (at a consequently heavier cost) police commitments to the community elsewhere must be affected by the concentration of such numbers in one place.

44. When upwards of 40,000 converge on a ground in a residential area the effect on the local community is very disagreeable. Large numbers of fans chant in the streets, often offensively. They invade gardens to urinate. Empty cans and other garbage are dropped in gardens, yards and in the street. Shops may be pillaged. Traffic is

congested or diverted. Streets are filled with parked coaches and cars. Side-streets are cordoned off by police to protect residents. Recently, a police cordon was thought necessary at a half mile radius round Highbury when Liverpool visited Arsenal. Residents had to establish their identity. The operation was successful in preventing disorder but the need to conduct such operations and the resultant disruption contributes to the poor image of football in the community at large.

What does Segregation Achieve?

45. Segregation, which is the main feature of present crowd control policy, aims only to contain and control bad behaviour, not to eliminate it. Indeed, the very fact that rival fans are separated tends to increase and polarise their hostility to each other. Segregation breeds an "us and them" attitude. The opposing supporters can be seen as a physically distinct group upon whom animosity can be focussed. Again, the knowledge that the "enemy" is physically restrained from violent riposte may encourage baiting and abuse which caution would otherwise deter. There is force too in the view that if people are herded and confined as potential offenders, that concept may in some cases become self-fulfilling. So, although segregation may have appeared the only way to maintain the excitement of the adversarial atmosphere at football grounds whilst keeping the peace, it merely controlled the symptoms of hooliganism. The disease remained and may even have been intensified by the segregation. Other games have not resorted to it. For example, there is no segregation at rugby league matches although the catchment sections of population, from which support is drawn both to football and rugby league, seem similar.

Who are the Hooligans?

46. In chapter 5 of his Final Report, Mr Justice Popplewell exploded three popular fallacies about hooliganism. First that it is something new; secondly, that it is only found at soccer matches and thirdly, that it is a specifically English disease. He went on to consider the nature of football hooliganism, the characteristics of the hooligan, possible causes of hooligan behaviour and experience in other countries. I do not propose to repeat his analysis. Nothing has thrown any doubt on it in the four years since he reported although much has been written by journalists, academics and others. I agree with him that there is no simple explanation for all the misbehaviour attached to football and there is no single remedy. It is important, however, to recognise the clear distinction between quite different groups of hooligans.

47. There are those who misbehave spontaneously in or around the ground in response to some perceived grievance – a goal against their team, a doubtful decision of a referee or taunting from others. But there are other groups who go out bent on causing trouble for its own sake. The latter were described by Mr Justice Popplewell as "the new hooligans". Often they hold down good jobs during the week, dress stylishly and detach themselves from those fans with club scarves who travel on official coaches or trains. They plan their violence as a recreation in itself to which the football is secondary or a mere background. Unfortunately, these groups can foment trouble and galvanise support from fans who would not otherwise misbehave. Thus the effect of the "new hooligans" can grow out of proportion to their numbers.

48. Mr Justice Popplewell summarised his conclusions as to the nature and motivation of hooligan groups at paragraph 5.90 of his Final Report as follows:-

"I (a) That there has always been a group, albeit a small group who find violence attractive; who currently find the football ground a convenient theatre for their violence and the football match the occasion for the display of their aggressive tendencies which on other days and at other times they will be exhibiting in public houses, the city centre or elsewhere. Their main target at football grounds is opposing fans. They choose to exercise that violence at a football match for a number of simple reasons. The date and place of a match are fixed; the nature of the opposition is known; its presence is certain, so is that of the police. Their own support is known. Its presence too is certain. The battle lines can be drawn. Thus plans can be made well in advance for the particular acts of violence that they intend to create.

(b) And while there is a good deal of academic support for the view that violence was at one time the prerogative of the so called "rough" working class that is no longer the complete picture today. A majority of today's hooligans no doubt do fit into that category, but some do not. They come from a variety of backgrounds, many have reasonable jobs and earn a proper living.

(c) Whether they are motivated by the same reasons as their predecessors can only be a matter of conjecture; there seems little reason however to believe otherwise.

II (a) A second group imitates the first element I have identified. Thus those not particularly given to violence witness violence in others and see it being exercised, without let or hindrance. People expect the spectators on the terraces to behave in an aggressive way and to use foul language. It then becomes accepted as the norm and thus becomes a part of the pattern of life which would not be tolerated elsewhere. This knock-on effect can be seen in violence in the streets of our cities, unconnected with football.

(b) The feeling of anonymity in the crowd gives rise to a loss of inhibition and self-discipline. The association with those of similar disposition, the enthusiasm and the partisan support for the team, which itself causes an atmosphere, all create a situation which can readily give rise to violence.

III Then there is a third group (not always separate from the other two groups) who cause violence for a reason, either real or supposed. It may be an inability quickly to get into the ground; it may be the presence of rival spectators in a part of the ground to which the fans think they have a claim.

IV Finally there are those, the vast majority of spectators, who abhor violence and wish only for an afternoon of pleasure at a football match."

The oral and written evidence I have received, the studies and reports I have read on the subject and my own observations lead me to agree entirely with that summary. I would add only one further element – alcohol.

Alcohol

49. There can be no doubt that an excited and volatile crowd is more difficult to control and more prone to disorder if it includes numbers who have been drinking. Drink is not a major factor affecting Mr Justice Popplewell's group I. Their violence tends to be planned coldly and soberly. But group II is often rendered disorderly and more readily imitates the violence of others because inhibitions are removed by drink. Likewise, group III responds to a grievance, is readier to take offence and reacts more impulsively and violently because of drink.

50. Drinking before matches increased in parallel with the growth of hooliganism. Before the 5 day week, those coming straight from work to the football ground on a Saturday had little time to drink excessively. During the 1960s and 1970s young men in their twenties acquired a new affluence and spending on drink increased. The advent of the supermarket with an off-licence provided numerous outlets for the sale of canned beer; so it became easy to have alcohol at the match and on the way to it, whether the local pubs were open or not. Finally, apart from time and liquor being available, there has developed an attitude to drinking in the UK not found to the same extent elsewhere – a cult of drinking to excess. The spectacle of young fans, tanked up with beer, whether near our own football grounds or (more damagingly to our reputation abroad) at foreign football stadia is all too familiar. Yet, for example in Italy, the largest wine producing country in Europe, football fans and indeed people generally do not drink to get drunk. Although they have their own brand of hooliganism (from the "Ultras" as they are known) alcohol is not a major factor. Here it certainly is and it remains so despite legislation banning sales or possession of alcohol in football grounds and the carrying of alcohol on public service and hired vehicles bound for such grounds.

Poor Leadership

51. The hierarchy inside football has a number of levels over and above the spectators. At the top is the national management of the game. In England the Football Association is responsible for the administration and welfare of all football down to the lowliest amateur club and football in schools. The Football League is a separate body with responsibility for the 92 professional League clubs. In Scotland and Wales there are equivalent bodies. Below that top management, each of the League clubs has its own Board of Directors. Then there are the referees, the managers and the players. Finally there are organisations representing the supporters – the Football Supporters' Association and the National Federation of Football Supporters' Clubs. One would have hoped that the upper echelons in this hierarchy would have taken a lead in securing reasonable safety and comfort for the spectators and in enforcing good behaviour by precept and example. Unfortunately, these hopes have not generally been realised and indeed at times poor examples have been set.

52. The FA and the FL have not seen it as their duty to offer guidance to clubs on safety matters. In their written submission they said:–

"Of course, both The FA and The Football League are concerned to ensure that crowd safety standards are the highest reasonably practicable. It is felt, however, that neither of these authorities should be charged with the responsibility of setting detailed safety standards or enforcing them."

They have been much concerned to avoid pitch invasions because they interfere with the smooth progress of the fixture list and incur criticism and penalties from the European football authorities. But advice, for example, as to turnstile lay outs, the division of viewing areas and, until recently, on ratios of seating to standing areas has not been forthcoming. As another specific example, in selecting Hillsborough as the venue for the Cup semi-final, the FA did not consider in any depth whether it was suitable for a high risk match with an attendance of 54,000 requiring to be segregated, all of whom were, in effect, away supporters lacking week in week out knowledge of the ground. No special inspection was made; no consultation with Sheffield Wednesday or the local authority took place.

53. As for the clubs, in some instances it is legitimate to wonder whether the directors are genuinely interested in the welfare of their grass-roots supporters. Boardroom struggles for power, wheeler-dealing in the buying and selling of shares and indeed of whole clubs sometimes suggest that those involved are more interested in the personal financial benefits or social status of being a director than of directing the club in the interests of its supporter customers. In most commercial enterprises, including the entertainment industry, knowledge of the customer's needs, his tastes and his dislikes is essential information in deciding policy and planning. But, until recently, very few clubs consulted to any significant extent with the supporters or their organisations.

54. Encouragement and indeed requirement of good behaviour by the fans should be a prime aim of club management. Here again positive leadership has often been lacking and on occasions counter-productive. It cannot help to promote good behaviour if a club chairman has his photograph in the programme presenting a cheque for £750 by way of recoupment to a club player fined that sum by the FA for misbehaviour on the pitch. The same applies to another chairman who extended a VIP welcome to home coming "supporters" convicted of misbehaviour whilst attending a match in Greece, even if he was sceptical as to the fairness of the criminal process.

55. Then there is what happens on the pitch itself. Long departed are Corinthian Casual standards; accepting decisions of the referee without demur; affecting a modest diffidence on scoring a sensational goal. For many years now referees' decisions have been regularly challenged by spread arms and entreaties; even an unsensational goal has caused the scorer to be hugged and embraced all the way back to the centre spot. The cool self-control of Corinthian Casuals will never return. Perhaps we should not lament its departure since there is no harm in a reasonable show of joy in success. But, more recently, things have gone further. On scoring a goal a player nowadays often rushes straight towards the perimeter fencing and either affects to climb it or, with fists raised and shaking, goes on his knees to excite response from supporters. Little has been done to stop such demonstrations which are calculated to hype up the fans into hysteria.

56. At the other extreme from demonstrations of joy and triumph, violence on the field of play by tackles aimed at opponents' legs, stamping, elbowing and holding is commonly to be seen. Until lately, the FA's response to such violence amongst players has been weak. Negligible fines on offenders, without penalty to the clubs either in fines or loss of points, have tended to discredit the FA's discharge of its disciplinary role. In the last couple of months, prompted by a series of much publicised incidents and by media criticism, a firmer line has at last been adopted. These incidents have involved violent conduct by players off the ball. At the end of the match between Norwich City and Arsenal on 4 November 1989, a number of players on both sides were involved in an incident when punches were exchanged. The referee said he was not going to make any report on the matter. The FA initially announced that if there was no report from the referee there was nothing they could do. However, wiser counsels prevailed; officials of the FA saw the incident on video and decided to take action. In the result Norwich City were fined £50,000 and Arsenal £20,000. Other incidents occurred within days at three other grounds involving violence on the field between players and, in one instance, managers.

57. To complete this survey of the present football malaise, it is necessary to mention the media. Football is highly newsworthy. For the World Cup, provision is being made at the San Siro stadium, Milan for no fewer than 5,000 journalists. In the domestic UK scene, the long haul throughout the season to become League champions or Cup winners is followed not only by the millions who actually attend matches but by many millions more via the media. They watch games and listen to the pundits endlessly discussing them on television; they read about them in the newspapers and they fill in the football pool coupons. So players and spectators are exposed to constant scrutiny. When scuffles or fights occur, whether on the field or on the terraces, they are inevitably witnessed by millions and such incidents of bad behaviour are aggregated into a reputation tarnishing the national game as a whole. When our supporters go to Europe, they are preceded by this reputation. It is expected they will behave badly, so whether they do so initially or not they are likely to meet a hostile reception from their counterparts. Thus incidents are provoked and the syndrome continues.

58. I have sought in the broadest terms to identify those features which disfigure football today. But despite them, and despite the decline in attendances from the peak years, the game still commands massive public support and interest. Indeed, in the last couple of years there has been some increase in attendances for reasons to be explored later. After the horror of Hillsborough and the analysis of football's troubles which it has prompted, the lesson is surely that now is the moment for the fullest reassessment of policy for the game. Accordingly, before considering detailed recommendations for securing a basic level of safety and for improving crowd control, I think it appropriate to consider how the low standards described in this chapter could be raised.

CHAPTER 2

A BETTER FUTURE FOR FOOTBALL

59. It is not enough to aim only at the minimum measures necessary for safety. That has been, at best, the approach in the past and too often not even that standard has been achieved. What is required is the vision and imagination to achieve a new ethos for football. Grounds should be upgraded. Attitudes should be more welcoming. The aim should be to provide more modern and comfortable accommodation, better and more varied facilities, more consultation with the supporters and more positive leadership. If such a policy is implemented it will not only improve safety. There will also be an improvement in behaviour, making crowd control easier.

60. At some clubs changes have already been made towards realising this new concept of how football should be. For example, at Ibrox Park, scene of the appalling disaster in 1971, there has been a total transformation. The old main stand remains and still has some standing areas in front of it. But three new stands have been built round the rest of the ground. They are colourful, convenient and are all-seating. They are constructed so as to provide a covered concourse at first floor level running the length of the stand. At the rear of that concourse throughout its length are modern lavatories for both sexes. At the front are attractive fast food service points offering a good range of food and drinks (but no alcohol). The walls are clean; the flooring is of studded rubber. Mounted overhead, at regular intervals of a few yards along the whole concourse, are television sets tuned to a sports programme giving information on the day's fixtures, excerpts from previous matches and general sports coverage. These arrangements encourage fans to arrive in good time, to have wholesome refreshments in a clean and pleasant setting, to enjoy on the television the kind of pre-match entertainment which genuinely interests them, to visit a decent toilet, and then to walk up a few steps to take their seats for the match. All of this is under cover and it is enjoyed not just by the affluent but by the ordinary supporter. Significantly, the facilities are not abused. Occasional graffiti do appear but are wiped away promptly and the overall impression is that if spectators are offered civilised conditions they come to respect them.

All-Seating

61. There is no panacea which will achieve total safety and cure all problems of behaviour and crowd control. But I am satisfied that seating does more to achieve those objectives than any other single measure.

62. It is obvious that sitting for the duration of the match is more comfortable than standing. It is also safer. When a spectator is seated he has his own small piece of territory in which he can feel reasonably secure. He will not be in close physical contact with those around him. He will not be jostled or moved about by swaying or surging. Small or infirm or elderly men and women as well as young children are not buffeted, smothered or unsighted by larger and more robust people as on the terraces. The seated spectator is not subject to pressure of numbers behind or around him during the match. He will not be painfully bent double over a crush barrier. Those monitoring numbers will know exactly how many are there without having to count them in or assess the density by visual impression. There will still, of course, be scope for crowd pressure on stairways whilst entering and especially when leaving, but involuntary and uncontrolled crowd movements occasioned by incidents in the game are effectively eliminated.

63. It is true that at moments of excitement seated spectators do, and may be expected to, rise from their seats. But the moment passes and they sit down again. I also recognise that seating is only regarded as more comfortable than standing if cover is provided. The consensus is that, although standing on an exposed terrace on a wet day is disagreeable, sitting in the rain is worse. So, increased seating does require that cover be provided.

64. Apart from comfort and safety, seating has distinct advantages in achieving crowd control. It is possible to have disturbances in a seated area and they have occurred, but with the assistance of CCTV the police can immediately zoom in with a camera and pinpoint the seats occupied by the trouble-makers as well as the trouble-makers themselves. Moreover, if numbered tickets are issued to named purchasers, the police have a further aid to identifying miscreants.

65. Numbered tickets matching numbered seats also help to identify forgeries. Forged tickets for standing areas may not be discovered. In the past, they simply led to inflated numbers on the terraces at all-ticket matches. But there can only be one valid ticket for each numbered seat and the existence of a forgery is immediately exposed.

66. The evidence I have received has been overwhelmingly in favour of more seating accommodation. At present, the ratio throughout the 92 League clubs in England and Wales is about two thirds standing to one third seated. But whilst most are in favour of reversing that ratio, there are those who wish to retain a proportion of standing room. Amongst them are the FA and the football supporters' organisations. Essentially they deploy three arguments.

67. The first is an emotional one based on a desire to retain the traditional culture derived from the close contact of the terraces. "My grandfather stood here; my father stood here with me; why shouldn't I stand here with my son?" is a commonly expressed view. Moreover, to many young men the camaraderie of singing together, jumping up and down, responding in unison to the naming of the players, their emergence on to the pitch, the scoring of a goal, an unpopular decision – all of these are an integral part of enjoying the match. They like being part of an amorphous seething crowd and do not wish to have each his own place in a seat.

68. The second argument is that conversion to all-seating will reduce the numbers of fans who can be admitted to the ground; so, many would-be spectators will be disappointed. This assumes a significantly greater density being permitted for standing places than for seating. It also assumes that the size of present crowds regularly exceeds projected all-seated capacity. But the FA's own evidence showed that during the 1988/89 season the number of occasions when attendances at League clubs exceeded projected all-seater capacity ranged from nil to 16. The 16 attendances were at Liverpool, who have accepted the need for all-seating. For only three clubs in the first and second divisions did the attendance exceed the projected all-seated capacity on more than 10 occasions, and for 21 out of 44 clubs in these two divisions the attendance never exceeded the projected all-seated capacity. In only one case (Liverpool) was the average attendance during the season in excess of the projected all-seated capacity.

69. Finally, cost. Spectators do not want to pay and, it is argued, many could not pay the substantially higher price of a seat as against the cost of standing.

70. I am not convinced that the cherished culture of the terraces is wholly lost when fans are seated. Watching the more boisterous and demonstrative sections at all-seater grounds, I have noted no absence of concerted singing, chanting, clapping or gesticulating in unison. The communal spirit is still there and finds ready expression. To such extent as the seating limits togetherness or prevents movement, that price is surely worth paying for the benefits in safety and control.

71. Moreover, the maximum density which experience now shows to be acceptable in standing areas tends to take the force out of the first two arguments. If standing density is little more than seating density, the melded mass previously found on terraces becomes more diffuse and the intensity of the togetherness becomes little greater standing than sitting. Likewise, at such a density, the difference between the admissible numbers standing and sitting become marginal. It can be made up by having two or more tiers of seating where previously there was only one tier of standing.

72. As to cost, clubs may well wish to charge somewhat more for seats than for standing but it should be possible to plan a price structure which suits the cheapest seats to the pockets of those presently paying to stand. At Ibrox, for example, seating is £6, standing £4 – not a prohibitive price or differential.

The Trend in the UK

73. The superior safety of seating has already persuaded a number of clubs in the UK to convert their terraces to seating either totally or predominantly. Following Hillsborough, Liverpool have announced their intention to adapt their famous Kop to seating. In Scotland, Aberdeen's ground at Pittodrie became all-seater in 1978; Clydebank followed suit; St Johnstone's new ground at Perth is all-seated. Wembley stadium will early in 1990 accommodate 80,000 spectators, all-seated.

74. Those opposed to all-seating point out that previous attempts to introduce it have met with spectator resistance. Coventry City was the first English club to install seating throughout its ground in 1981. In 1983 the club reverted to allowing 2,000 to stand. In 1985, after visiting fans of Manchester City tore up seats and used them as missiles, the ground reverted to standing. Queen's Park Rangers also moved towards all-seated accommodation but removed some seats under pressure from supporters.

75. Since then, however, Hillsborough has happened; thinking has changed; responsible comment by government, football authorities and media has prepared the way for change. Moreover, there are now seats available which cannot be manually torn and used as missiles. Those at Utrecht, for example, have survived intact for seven years despite usage and deliberate experimental tests of their strength.

76. It is possible that in the early stages of conversion there may be instances of fans standing on the seats or in front of them because they are used to standing or in order to register a protest, but I am satisfied that in England and Wales as in Scotland and abroad spectators will become accustomed and educated to sitting. The evidence I have received shows that more recently, where seating has been installed, the fans have come to accept and like it. At Ibrox Park, for example, the seated areas are the most popular and tickets for them sell in preference to those for standing. Significantly, trouble from misbehaviour and physical injuries have been reduced since most of the crowd became seated. Such trouble and accidental injuries as still occur are primarily in the remaining standing areas. It is planned to convert them to seating in the near future.

Sir Norman Chester Centre Research

77. The Sir Norman Chester Centre for Football Research, attached to the University of Leicester, is funded by the Football Trust. In November 1989 the Centre undertook a survey of registered members of the Football Supporters' Association to discover the views of committed football fans on a number of the issues after Hillsborough which are covered in my Report. The extension of seating was one such issue. Numerous questions were asked on a number of different hypotheses. The Report states that substantial majorities in the sample were in favour of maintaining the status quo on the seats/terraces balance at their own clubs. However, the Report continues:

"53.6% claimed they would actually support the drive for more seating (sic) if they were reasonably priced and covered. The addition of these last two points – concessions on price and cover – also seemed to have dramatic effects in reducing levels of opposition to the prospects of all-seated facilities as we shall see later".

When all-seating was put to the sample there was a majority against it, but the Report goes on:

"Finally, and perhaps significantly, opposition in our sample to the introduction of all-seated facilities diminishes considerably when one introduces provisos on price and protection from the elements. When this is done, more people in our sample support all-seaters than oppose them."

Europe

78. The trend towards seating is even stronger in Europe and is now being driven by decrees of both national and European football authorities.

79. In Italy the imminence of the 1990 World Cup competition has forced the pace of progress. The Italian Ministry of the Interior decreed on 25 August 1989 that for open air facilities with a capacity of more than 10,000 spectators at football games and for covered ones with a capacity of more than 4,000 spectators no standing will be allowed after 30 April 1990. Those facilities must have only numbered seats each not less than 0.45 metres wide. The San Siro stadium in Milan will by then seat 85,000 spectators; the Olimpico stadium in Rome will seat 87,000.

80. In Holland, Utrecht's ground built in 1982 has seating for 12,000 and standing room for 8,000. The club already intended to convert the latter to seating. However, on 6 December 1989 the Dutch equivalent of the FA (the KNVB) agreed with the Dutch clubs to cut the standing capacity of football grounds by 10% each year over the next decade so as to render football stadia in the Netherlands in effect all-seater at the end of the 1990s.

81. In following this phasing Holland's policy is in accord with a resolution presently under consideration by UEFA (Union des Associations Européennes de Football). The resolution proposes that for the 1990/91 season only 80% of the standing tickets may be sold, that figure to be reduced every season by 10% until 1999.

82. FIFA (Fédération Internationale de Football Association) passed a resolution on 26 July 1989 providing that as from the preliminary competition for the 1994 World Cup (starting in autumn 1992) "matches may in principle only be played in all-seater stadia". The resolution went on "as from 1993 it will be the duty of the Confederations and National Associations to hold high-risk matches in their zones only in all-seater stadia." High-risk matches are defined under UEFA Regulations as follows:

"I All UEFA final and semi-final ties of the UEFA club competitions as well as final tournament matches of the European Football Championship.

II When declared as such by UEFA on the basis of previous incidents of supporters of one or both teams or of other exceptional considerations.

14

III When it is expected that visiting team supporters will exceed 10% of stadium capacity or will exceed 3,000 persons.

IV When full capacity stadium is expected or more than 50,000 spectators present.

V When the match is likely to attract a large number of emigrants/foreign workers originating from the country of the visiting team, who live either in the country where the match is being played or in neighbouring countries."

Thus world and European football authorities are clearly determined to enforce the conversion of stadia to all-seating, so far as international matches and other matches under their control are concerned. It is true that their resolutions will not be binding in regard to League or domestic football matches. But they are a pointer in the direction of safety and control and as such have been emulated by Italy and Holland domestically.

83. Furthermore, I am told by the FA that they regard themselves as duty bound to follow, in the domestic football scene, any Resolution passed by FIFA although strictly such Resolution is binding only in international matches or matches between UK clubs and clubs from abroad. Thus, the FA regard the Resolution of 26 July 1989 as effective in relation to the League, Cup and other domestic fixtures from 1993 onwards. The Resolution does not force clubs to install all-seating as a condition of staging high-risk matches. There is still the option to use only those parts of the ground which have seating. Clearly, unless these are substantial, attendance will be much reduced. One would therefore expect the major clubs to adapt their grounds to accommodate the maximum seating they can manage by the time the Resolution takes effect. Smaller and more impecunious clubs may prefer to postpone conversion. However, if a small club with little seating accommodation draws a large first division club at home in the Cup in 1993 (a high-risk match) it will be able only to use its limited seating accommodation or the game will have to be played at a better equipped ground elsewhere.

The Football Spectators Act 1989

84. The intention to follow this same trend was stated by your predecessor, Mr Douglas Hurd, in a statement to the House of Commons two days after Hillsborough. He added:–

"This would involve the disappearance of terraces at (major) grounds. It might also involve amendments to strengthen the Football Spectators Bill so that its provisions for the licensing of grounds matched this concept".

In the event, machinery for implementing increased seating is to be found in section 11 of the 1989 Act. There, provision is made for the Football Licensing Authority (set up under section 8) to be directed by the Secretary of State to include in any licence to admit spectators a condition imposing requirements as respects the seating of spectators at designated football matches at the premises; "and it shall be the duty of the authority to comply with the direction".

Association Football only or Designated Grounds?

85. In considering seating and standing, I have concentrated so far on association football because it attracts the largest and most volatile crowds and has been troubled with misbehaviour. But should recommendations about seating be confined to association football or should they go further? Wherever a line is drawn complaint may be made that it is illogical, but two possibilities seem more logical than most; either to confine recommendations to the 92 clubs in the Football League or to apply them to grounds designated under the 1975 Act as amended. The latter course would include a number of Rugby League, Rugby Union and cricket grounds. I acknowledge that so far, happily, misbehaviour at those grounds has been minimal. However, even leaving aside possible misbehaviour, where there are large numbers there is a risk of overcrowding. A well attended Rugby match of either code may attract numbers in excess of those attending many Football League matches. There would seem little reason for requiring a fourth division League club to convert to seating whilst permitting major Rugby clubs to keep their terraces indefinitely.

86. On the other hand, proposals for all-seating would clearly be inappropriate in relation to sports events at which spectators are accustomed, and should be entitled, to move about. For example, at horserace meetings, spectators may wish to view horses in the paddock, place bets, view races from different vantage points and enjoy the other facilities of what is a social occasion as well as a sports event. Other examples of events at which spectators move about and should be free to do so are greyhound racing and golf tournaments.

87. The criteria for designating a sports ground under the 1975 Act as amended are laid down in section 1(1):

"The Secretary of State may by order designate as a sports ground requiring a certificate under this Act (in this Act referred to as a "safety certificate") any sports ground which in his opinion has accommodation for more than 10,000 spectators."

Section 1(1)(A) permits the Secretary of State to substitute such other number as he considers appropriate for the number 10,000.

88. Clearly the purpose of such designation is to bring safety of grounds with capacity for substantial numbers under the control of the local authority. Whilst some grounds with a capacity of more than 10,000 may currently have an average attendance of only say 3,000, there is always the prospect of a visit from a large club, an attractive Cup draw, or an upturn in fortunes bringing in larger crowds. Safety provisions must be capable of coping with such events. Indeed, danger is more likely to result if there is an occasional match with a large attendance than if such matches were regular since those controlling it and those attending it will be inexperienced.

89. For these reasons, I think recommendations to increase seating should be applied to all designated grounds. I appreciate that the machinery provided in section 11 of the Football Spectators Act 1989 can be used only to regulate the extension of seating at association football grounds. However, the Secretary of State has power under section 6(2) of the 1975 Act, as amended, to provide for securing safety by regulations and may prescribe terms and conditions to be inserted in Safety Certificates under section 15A as indicated in the next chapter. These powers could be used, even without the provision in section 11 of the 1989 Act, to prescribe mandatory rules about seating. So, by a combination of his 1989 Act powers and his 1975 Act powers or solely by exercising the latter, the Secretary of State can require the progressive extension of seating at designated grounds.

90. **I therefore conclude and recommend that designated grounds under the 1975 Act should be required in due course to be converted to all-seating.** I do so for the compelling reasons of safety and control already set out; also, so far as association football is concerned, because the present trend at home and abroad and the rules of the world and European football authorities make the move to all-seating irresistible.

Phasing

91. Unless some time factors are specified, progress towards all-seating may well be protracted. This is recognised in the phasing proposed in the UEFA Resolution quoted above and in the machinery set up in section 11 of the Football Spectators Act 1989.

92. **For high-risk association football matches I welcome and endorse the adoption by the FA of the FIFA Resolution requiring no standing tickets to be sold after 1993 and its application to domestic fixtures.**

93. As to other matches, I consider that without the impetus locally of the World Cup, which is the spur for speedy change in Italy, and having regard to the present state of our grounds, it would be asking too much to require conversion in the UK in the next two or three years. **For all grounds designated under the 1975 Act except for first division and second division League grounds, and national stadia, I think a timing along the lines suggested in the Resolution under consideration by UEFA (and now adopted in Holland) is reasonable *ie* that standing tickets should be reduced by 10% per year starting with a 10% deduction effective from August 1990 and so be phased out by August 1999.**

94. **However, I recommend that grounds in the first and second divisions of the League and national stadia should be all-seated by the start of the 1994/1995 season.** It is at those grounds that the larger crowds attend and, in the interests of both safety and crowd control, I consider they should have seating for all spectators in five years rather than ten years. **The reduction in standing tickets should therefore be at 20% per annum from August 1990 and be complete by August 1994. Any club promoted to the second division of the League should be given a reasonable period in which to comply. A similar approach should be adopted in Scotland.**

Planning Ground Improvements

95. Increased seating and other ground improvements will require expert planning and much finance. As to planning, it is crucial that before clubs embark upon major work, they should have the best information and advice on modern ground design. Conversion to seating cannot necessarily be achieved merely by fixing seating onto existing terraces. For example, sight-lines, access to seats, gangways, roof cover and other factors

may require more extensive changes to the layout. Some clubs may be able wholly to redevelop their existing grounds; others may be limited by space, finance or crowd needs to more modest alterations. In some instances, the best course would be to move to a new site either alone or in conjunction with another club. Ultimate decisions on these options must be for the club management. No doubt, some of the bigger clubs will be able to engage the foremost contractors in this field to advise them and carry out the work. But even for them, and certainly for the lesser clubs, it would be of great value to have a body fully apprised of the latest developments in ground design, capable of giving expert advice on possible schemes and on ways and means of achieving them.

An Advisory Design Council

96. **I therefore support the suggestion of Professor Maunder's Technical Working Party that there should be established an Advisory Design Council to fulfil this role. It should, in my view, be set up by the FA and the FL whose functions should include offering a service of this kind to the clubs.** By way of analogy, in Italy this function is exercised by the Comitato Olimpico Nazionale Italiano (CONI). After studying many grounds, including those in Madrid, Vienna and Athens, CONI produced an excellent pamphlet on "Design Criteria for Safe Comfortable and Large Sports Facilities" supported by detailed studies showing how they can be achieved. These, together with models which may be inspected at CONI's headquarters in Rome, show how a modern stadium can be designed from car park to pitch so as to secure safety and crowd control.

Research

97. It has come to my attention only recently that the Sports Council published in 1981 a "Handbook of Sport and Recreational Building Design", and in 1989, a work entitled "Arenas, a Planning, Design and Management Guide". The 1981 work included, in volume three, studies on outdoor sports stadia. The 1989 work concentrated on indoor stadia. It seems that neither of these works was sent to the FA or the FL, nor have they acquired them. Again, in July 1986, the Institution of Structural Engineers formed an ad hoc committee "to bring together all current technical knowledge relevant to the appraisal of sports grounds and their individual elements. The committee's task was to establish a fully referenced body of knowledge within three years which would be complementary to the 'Guide to Safety at Sports Grounds'." The ad hoc committee has prepared a fifth draft of its report which will be finalised after the recommendations in my Report have been considered.

98. It is highly desirable that such worthwhile research as I have mentioned should all be brought together to achieve maximum benefit. With a formidable building and conversion programme for football grounds ahead, an Advisory Design Council set up by the FA and FL could make the best use of all available research here and abroad to assist and advise clubs.

Finance

99. The scale of the changes I recommend will necessarily require heavy expenditure, albeit over an extended period. It is not my function to make detailed proposals for financing the work. That is for football management and essentially for the clubs. However, lest it be thought that I have made proposals regardless of feasible funding, I ought to indicate sources and methods of finance which should make the improvements practicable, and some of the fiscal arguments which have been addressed to me.

The Football Trust (FT) and the Football Grounds Improvement Trust (FGIT)

100. Assistance in financing safety measures is presently available from the FT and the FGIT. The former is funded by the three major pools companies (Littlewoods, Vernons and Zetters) from the "Spot the Ball" Competition, at the rate of 21% of turnover, yielding over £9 million a year. The total given to British football since 1958 now approaches £120 million. The Trustees are empowered to use their funds to promote measures for the control or suppression of unruly behaviour in relation to football; to assist clubs to meet the obligations of the Safety of Sports Grounds Act 1975; to improve grounds and facilities for those who play and watch the game and for any other purpose they consider to be a benefit to the game of football in Great Britain and Northern Ireland. The FT allocates just over half its income (ie over £4.5 million) to assisting expenditure by League clubs on ground safety and improvements. This is done through the FGIT, a second independent trust. The FGIT was established in 1975, the arrangements being modified later in 1979 when the FT was brought into being.

101. Although it helps to fund many other works, from those at international grounds down to those at the lowliest clubs, the Trust continues to give first priority to assisting expenditure essential to the grant of a Safety Certificate for a designated ground. Under its trust deed, the FGIT is able to make grants of up to 75% of the total cost available to clubs carrying out work as a necessary condition of their being given a Safety

Certificate under the 1975 Act. Accordingly, should my recommendation of mandatory increases in seating be made a condition of the Safety Certificate, the work would be eligible for a grant from the FGIT.

102. However, even at £4.5 million a year, the FGIT fund would be insufficient. Additional financial requirements fell upon the League clubs on the implementation of the 1975 Act and still more after the fire at Bradford City's ground in May 1985. By February 1988 over £37 million had been paid out in grants. Pressures on finance led to the suspension of improvement grants in June 1987. The FGIT was able to reintroduce improvement grant aid on a limited basis during the closed season of 1988. However, the range of works required to upgrade the League grounds inevitably means that resources of the FGIT would be spread quite thinly. They will not be sufficient to finance the kind of improvements I have suggested, but the Trust provides a structure for doing so. By way of example, Sheffield Wednesday received a grant of £595,000 for the improvement of the Kop end at Hillsborough. This was in addition to some £431,000 given to the club for a total of 21 safety projects between September 1978 and October 1988. Even so, funds of this order will be insufficient to build new all-seated stands. How then, can additional revenue be generated?

Fiscal Considerations

103. Three arguments have been addressed to me by the football authorities suggesting alterations in tax structure to make funds available for ground improvements. Fiscal policy is for government and ultimately Parliament to decide, not for a judge. All I can usefully do is to set out the arguments.

(a) *VAT on the Spot the Ball Competition*

104. The Football Trust have suggested that if VAT were abolished on receipts from this competition, some £5 to £6 million would be available. This would amount to a direct subsidy from the Treasury. It would be contrary as I understand it not only to present government thinking but to long established principles of fiscal policy. If that is so, a different and perhaps more propitious approach would be for the FA to urge the Pool Promoters Association (PPA) to increase their contribution as part of a strategy to ensure the healthy development of the game from which the PPA makes its money.

(b) *Pool Betting Tax*

105. A second case made by the FA is for a reduction in Pool Betting Tax now standing at 42.5%. The suggestion is a reduction to 40% which would yield some £16 million. This, it is said, could be passed on to assist ground improvements in one of two ways: either the Government could continue to tax pool betting at the current level but make a donation to football equivalent to 2.5% of the tax recovered, or it could reduce the tax rate to 40% on the strict understanding that present proposals as to how any reduction of the 42.5% might be used were amended to allow football to derive the entire benefit from the money thus saved by the pool companies.

106. The FA seek to support their argument by reference to the structure of tax on horse racing. They claim the comparison shows football to be unfairly treated. In horse racing, the duty on off-course betting is 8%; on-course betting is not now taxed. There is a Horserace Betting Levy which goes to the improvement and maintenance of race courses. However, the comparison between football pools and racing is not of like with like. The relationship of stakes to winnings is different. The Football League presently receives £14 million a year from the PPA for the use of its fixture list. There is no payment similar to this in racing. Nor is there an equivalent in racing to the Football Trust or the FGIT. The Horserace Betting Levy is essentially based on voluntary agreement and is not regarded by the Treasury as a tax. There could be no basis for a levy on football pools unless there were agreement between the PPA and the Football League.

107. For these amongst other reasons, the racing analogy may not add weight to the FA's argument on pool betting tax. However, apart from that analogy, the FA submit there is a strong case for some reduction of the 42.5% tax. The Chester Report of 1968 recommended the establishment of a football levy. The Rothschild Royal Commission on Gambling recommended in 1977 a reduction in the pool betting tax from the level at that time of 40% to 37% to establish a levy board. The FA and the FL do not favour the creation of a football levy board. They consider that the Football Trust and the FGIT are appropriate bodies to receive and administer any money accruing to football were a reduction made in the pool betting tax. I can only say that the case for a modest reduction in the pool betting tax which convinced the Rothschild Commission in 1977 is arguably stronger now that the rate stands at 42.5%. It must in general be for commercial undertakings to be self-financing. This applies throughout the entertainment industry of which football clubs are a part. The football authorities appreciate and accept that they must find the necessary funding substantially from their own resources. Nevertheless, if grounds all over the country are to be upgraded and in some instances re-located so as to achieve safety for spectators, improvement in the quality of life for residents near grounds

and a reduction in the expensive police commitment to controlling matches, it can be argued there is a case for financial assistance, if not by direct subsidy then by some tax reduction.

108. Whether or not the FA's argument for tax reduction finds favour, there may well be scope for reassessing and possibly increasing the contribution made by pools to football. It would not matter whether such contribution is to be by voluntary levy, by an increase in the present percentage rate on receipts from the Spot the Ball Competition or by increasing the amount paid for the use of the fixture list.

(c) *Capital Allowances*

109. Complaint is made that no capital allowances can be claimed against tax in respect of ground improvements.

110. When asked why they seem ready and able to spend large sums, sometimes into millions of pounds, for a single player in preference to spending money on improving their grounds, the clubs usually give two reasons.

111. First, the attendance and satisfaction of their supporters depends essentially on success; so buying a brilliant player has priority over ground improvement.

Transfer Fees

112. They say the popular perception of transfer fees as excessive and extravagant is mistaken. The money, I was told again and again, simply circulates round the League clubs. It is calculated to bring on budding players. The level of payments is high, but it is forced up by prices continental clubs with huge financial backing (like Juventus from Fiat) are able to pay.

113. The "circulation" argument runs like this. First division club A buys an ace player for £1 million from club B. This enables club B to buy three players at, say, £250,000 each from three other clubs, C, D and E. Clubs C, D and E each buy two up-and-coming but not yet arrived players from lesser clubs for perhaps £100,000 each. So the process and the prices continue downwards eventually enabling the poorer clubs to keep going by cashing in on players they have trained from scratch. Meanwhile, to finance their £1 million purchase, club A may sell two or three players who are past their best to lower division clubs. This analysis may well have some validity, but there are notable exceptions. For example, when a French club bought a player from an English club for over £4 million the money had not been circulating round the League clubs.

A Levy on Transfer Fees?

114. Even if the "circulation" argument has some validity, the fact remains that transfer fees have reached a level which many regard as grotesque and certainly out of all proportion to the amounts spent on ground improvement. There is a case for the football authorities imposing a levy on such fees, the proceeds going to the FGIT to fund ground improvements. I suggest consideration be given to this.

Tax "Anomaly"

115. Secondly (and this is the tax argument) football clubs have a strong fiscal inducement to spend on players rather than ground improvements. Payments for players are allowable revenue expenditure. Improvements to the ground are not. In *Brown (Inspector of taxes) v Burnley Football and Athletic Company Ltd* 1983 AER 244, it was held that expenditure on a new stand to replace an old unsafe one did not qualify as an allowable deduction whether as a repair or as provision of plant. It is arguable that a fiscal provision which penalises the redevelopment of grounds whilst encouraging the payment of huge transfer fees is an anomaly, that it sends the wrong signals to clubs, and that it encourages them to neglect questions of safety in favour of promoting success on the field. To accede to this argument might fall foul of the maxim that hard cases make bad law. But as a matter of policy, it is argued that the encouragement of expenditure on ground improvements by a fiscal concession may well bear re-examination.

Club Financing

116. Whatever may come from the Pool Promoters Association via the two Trusts, or from any tax concession, in the end the bulk of the finances for ground improvement must be raised by the clubs themselves. Here, clubs are at a disadvantage compared with their European counterparts. On the continent most grounds are owned by local authorities which lease them to the clubs. They are regarded as providing a communal facility and often the stadium is available for a variety of sports and other functions; sports facilities and offices are built into the stadium complex.

117. Nevertheless, there are ways of financing improvements if the club management is enterprising and resourceful. Sponsorship is one. Presently it brings £17.5 million into football annually. Advertising on electric score boards and on hoardings round the ground as well as on tickets, programmes and membership cards is another. Associated companies marketing sports wear and other merchandise with the club's logo, the sale of television rights, the issue of debentures, and the sale of shares to the public are other methods which can be and have been used. In particular, I would expect the football authorities to seek the highest possible price for television rights. Under current contractual arrangements, the Football Association receives some £6 million pa from the sale of television rights for domestic broadcasts, of which some £2.5 million is distributed to clubs. They also receive between £0.75 million and £1 million for the sale of television rights overseas. Separate arrangements apply at Wembley. The Football League contracted some two years ago to sell the television rights for League matches for £11 million, linked to the Retail Price Index. The television companies know that football on the screen has a vast following. They should be expected to pay a substantial price for the rights to relay popular matches. For their part, the football authorities should ensure that this valuable source of revenue is directed towards improving stadia as a high priority.

118. The cost of covered seating throughout the 92 clubs in the Football League has been investigated by the FA. Whilst the assessment can only be a rough estimate and is subject to fluctuations due to inflation and other factors, the consultants suggested that to install seating throughout all the grounds might cost about £30 million. To provide cover over all those areas could cost a further £100 million. It should be noted, however, that no breakdown of that figure is given. Moreover, it assumes "all existing uncovered standing capacity should become covered". Given current attendances, it would seem unnecessary that all that capacity should be covered. In many instances, attendances are always well below the permitted capacity of the ground. In those cases, a much smaller scale solution involving the rebuilding or redevelopment of only part of the ground would be sufficient. There would be little point in providing covered seating accommodation throughout a ground if there is no realistic possibility of more than half of it being used. Costs may therefore be less daunting for the smaller clubs than the consultants' estimates suggest.

Upgraded Stadia or New Stadia

119. At major grounds where substantial resources can be generated, vast improvements can be made on existing sites if there is sufficient space. I have seen a number of imaginative examples of ground redevelopment. It has been achieved at Ibrox Park and is in the course of being achieved at Old Trafford, White Hart Lane and Hampden Park, to give only four examples.

120. However, I agree with the evidence from the Sports Council as to the need for space to facilitate car parking, external and internal circulation and sufficient exits and entrances to the spectator areas. They said:–

"The location of many existing football grounds in central city or town sites precludes this provision (of space) which implies the adoption of a gradual but progressive policy of disposing of grounds in densely developed areas and replacing the facility on the urban periphery. The Council believes that opportunities exist for such developments on a self-funding basis in many instances. This would also provide the opportunity for more than one club to be based at newly developed stadia constructed to a high specification and built to meet new demands for safety and comfort".

St Johnstone

121. I was impressed by the way this had been done at three particular grounds. At St Johnstone in Scotland, the solution has been to involve private capital directly. The ASDA supermarket chain bought the site of the old St Johnstone Football Club in the centre of Perth, redeveloped it as a supermarket, and built the club a brand new all-seated stadium for 10,000 spectators on the outskirts of the town. The site was, in effect, donated by a local farmer. It is close to a motorway exit and provides for extensive car parks. I accept that this confluence of factors might not be easy to reproduce elsewhere. In particular, land prices in some areas would be prohibitive and planning permission very difficult to obtain. A greenfield site is likely to be in a conservation or green belt area and the choice of sites is limited by the need to make the ground accessible to townsfolk albeit outside the town.

Utrecht

122. I saw two examples abroad where these problems had been tackled resolutely. At Utrecht an old stadium on the outskirts of the town was totally redeveloped on the same site ostensibly at nil cost. The contracting company which rebuilt the stadium (Ballast Nedam) is now in consultation with 11 clubs in England and Scotland with a view to building similar projects in partnership with the Football Association

and British Aerospace of which it is a subsidiary. Their concept involves the recognition that in the past, for all but a handful of days in the year, a stadium complex has usually and wastefully lain deserted. At Utrecht the stadium is owned by the municipality. The space underneath the stands and in the corners of the ground has been developed to provide accommodation for commercial use. The rent provides the municipality with sports accommodation which pays for itself. Some 6,000 square metres of commercial working areas and 24,000 square metres of commercial offices have been incorporated into the complex. The commercial uses of this accommodation include office accommodation, snack bars, sports facilities, photocopying and office equipment services, a driving school and a hairdresser. The large parking area is used except on match days as a "park and ride" facility for those working in the more congested areas of the city. The advantages for business are that shops and offices enjoy a prestigious high profile address with all necessary services and facilities. For the community, the commercial stadium serves as an arena both for trade and recreation. Appendix 5 is a photograph showing the stadium with the commercial infill in the corners and out into the car park.

Nimes

123.   The stadium at Nimes in Southern France is also owned by the municipality . It was built recently on the outskirts of the town with extensive parking and good access to road communications. The cost was some £17 million of which £16 million came from the municipality itself. The justification for this expenditure of public funds is the belief that the stadium is a communal asset. It provides not only a stadium for football or rugby but an extensive range of other sports facilities built into the complex. These include a gymnastic hall capable of hosting international matches, an "omnisport" hall for tennis, basket-ball and volley-ball, a judo hall, facilities for fencing and billiards, and a large exhibition hall which, at the time of our visit, had just been used for a car sales exhibition.

Local Authority Assistance

124.   All these three stadia are on a comparatively small scale. St Johnstone seats 10,000. Utrecht accommodates 20,000 and Nimes about 28,000. I accept that in the current financial climate and with our different approach to communal funding, local authorities are unlikely to be able to provide subsidies for such stadia, although local authorities do subsidize, for example, swimming baths, theatres and other leisure facilities which may serve fewer of their citizens. However, clubs which wish to move from centre town sites to new sites on the outskirts of town may well be able to find a purchaser as St Johnstone did with ASDA. Likewise, those who wish either to build a new stadium on the outskirts or to redevelop their stadium in town may be able to do so in a way which incorporates space for commercial lettings.

125.   In such situations, although the local authority may be unable to assist with finance, it could play a useful role in bringing parties together and as planning authority. It could take a favourable view, for example, of a planning application which involved the provision not only of a communal sports stadium but of further facilities, whether for sport or otherwise, benefitting the community as a whole. There has recently been a number of attempts by clubs to find greenfield sites for new grounds only to be turned down at each attempt on planning grounds. Clearly, an application for a football ground in a conservation area or green belt poses planning problems. But, although the protection of such areas is an important principle, two other considerations may also carry weight. First, that the quality of life of residents living adjacent to a football ground in a town would be much improved by resiting it elsewhere. Secondly, that if we want safety and improved standards at grounds there are some clubs which will need a new site at which to achieve them. To this end, local authorities should surely give what assistance they properly can. One useful example of the mutual assistance which a club and a local authority can give each other is an agreement made between Millwall and the London Borough of Lewisham. The latter agreed to pay £70,000 a year to the club which for its part agreed inter alia to make the ground available for various activities beneficial to the local community.

Ground Sharing

126.   Whether or not income-earning facilities are incorporated into a sports ground, it seems uneconomic that the stadium itself should be used by only one club, in effect once a fortnight. The cost to each club both of upgrading or building a stadium and of maintaining it could be halved if sensible sharing arrangements could be made. But there is resistance to this. A number of cities have two clubs, each with its own ground. Such is local rivalry that the idea of ground sharing seems anathema to many. Yet, faced with the expense of seating and ground improvement, it would make financial sense. Opposition to sharing an entirely new ground may be marginally less than to one club sharing another's existing ground. Recently Mr Peter Robinson, Chief Executive of Liverpool FC, was quoted as saying:

"If someone were to build a high-quality stadium on Merseyside, we and Everton would be quite happy to share it – even though the idea might not appeal to the fans at first".

If two clubs could sell their inner city grounds with planning permission, the resultant capital would go a long way to building a modern shared stadium on a more suitable site.

127. It works abroad. AC Milan and Inter Milan share the San Siro stadium. In Turin, Juventus and Torino also share. Genova and Sampdoria provide a third example.

128. As long ago as 1981, in the Sports Council's Handbook of Sports and Recreational Building Design, Volume Three (Outdoor Sports), ground-sharing was considered in a technical study of stadia. The author, Mr Faulkner Brown, wrote at page 24:–

"Several courses would appear to be open to football clubs. One is that they might rationalise their position and, wherever possible, jointly use a single stadium. This could happen at Sheffield, Nottingham and Bristol. Fulham could move in with Chelsea and Brentford with Queen's Park Rangers. Inter-Milan and AC Milan, for all their deep rivalry, do live happily enough together in the giant San Siro stadium. The British clubs could all retain their identity, halve their overheads and realise handsomely the value of their freehold properties, if they could cope with their fiercely held views of club individuality and club pride.

Another alternative would be, where possible, for clubs to offer unused land adjacent to the stadium for development and, in realising the assets from the land, to plough them back into the cost of stadium reconstruction. This, of course, has happened at Lord's and is having some noticeable effects at the Oval and in other county cricket grounds.

A further alternative is to build additional sports facilities alongside the stadium, not necessarily in emulation of the ancient Greek example (but nevertheless there is a parallel), so that a large number of sports clubs could use all the facilities. This scheme has been developed to some extent both in the United States and on the continent."

Super-Stadia

129. So far, I have referred only to club grounds. But there is a case for having a small number of super-stadia capable of accommodating very large crowds for international matches or major Cup ties. At present, the only such stadium in the UK is Wembley which will accommodate 80,000 all-seated. Like Wembley, any other stadia of large capacity could be available not only for football but for other sports, for pop concerts and other large events.

130. A consortium comprising British Aerospace, the FA and Ballast Nedam (who built the Utrecht stadium) is presently considering the building of a new national stadium at Birmingham to accommodate 100,000. There is a suggestion that this project, if carried through, would provide a replacement for Wembley. However, it may well be that there is room for both. This would give a venue in London and a venue in the Midlands for major events. Hampden Park has served as Scotland's international football ground for many years and when planned improvements are complete it should continue to do so. It is arguable that one more large stadium may be required in the north of England but the upgrading of a ground such as Old Trafford might well suffice to achieve this purpose.

Leadership and Example

131. I turn from stadia and money to one aspect of football which gives wide scope for improvement at very little cost. Much is written about the misbehaviour of spectators; but misbehaviour is often imitative. Hooligans in the crowd find others who will copy them. Similarly, incitement from the pitch or bad behaviour by players has a malign influence on the crowd. For many fervent followers, the men on the pitch are heroes to be revered and emulated. After a goal, when the scorer demonstrates to the fans behind the fencing, the resultant surge forward and hysteria is bad for safety and bad for crowd control. It should not occur. Worse still, when players fight, the fans follow suit. Lest anyone doubt this, the recent examples of fighting between players bear it out. In two of the four incidents in November 1989, crowd misbehaviour resulted directly from fighting between players. At Highbury, fans came out on to the pitch to join in. At Upton Park, scuffles between Wimbledon and West Ham players provoked surging, fighting and coin throwing on the terraces.

132. It is in the first instance up to the players themselves, then the referees, the managers and the club directors to stop both incitement and violence by players whether on or off the ball. The referees, managers and directors have power to do this. If and when they fail to use it, the FA must take a firm disciplinary line using their very full powers to fine those involved including the clubs and to penalise the clubs in points. If all else fails, there is no reason why violence on the pitch should have any immunity from the law of the land or from police action.

133. On the positive side, management could do much to create a better atmosphere in the grounds by what they say and what they write in programmes and magazines. By consulting with supporters they could enlist the goodwill and help of the decent majority to isolate and rebuff misbehaviour from the minority rather than imitate it. A campaign for better behaviour could be launched by the clubs through their literature and backed by managers and players using their popular hero appeal.

134. I should add that violence on the pitch is not confined to soccer. There has been a growing incidence of stampings and punchings in Rugby Union games even at the highest level. Reaction from referees, clubs and even international selectors has tended to play such incidents down. Although spectator behaviour has not, as yet, been adversely affected by such incidents, the authorities ought to deal firmly with them before that happens and in any event, simply because violence should be put down.

Family and Membership Areas

135. Much progress has been made at a number of clubs recently in bringing women and children back to watching football by creating separate family areas. Similarly, partial membership schemes have enabled clubs to reserve parts of the ground exclusively to members. This has had the dual advantage of creating areas of reliable good behaviour and offering discounts, favourable travel facilities and other benefits to members. The good behaviour depends on those who pay for membership being more likely to be responsible and upon their risking loss of membership if they transgress.

136. At a number of grounds, family areas have been de-segregated in the sense that families drawn from away supporters have been permitted to share family areas with home supporters. I have already indicated how segregation has tended to worsen hostility between rival fans. It is difficult once segregation has been practised to dispense with it, certainly at a stroke. These joint family areas may prove to be the first step in a retreat from segregation. If the process can be extended gradually to allowing members of the visiting club to share the membership area of the home club, useful progress will have been made. It will be made easier if there is seating rather than standing.

The Disabled

137. I received evidence from the Royal Association for Disability and Rehabilitation (RADAR) and the Access Committee for England drawing attention to the opportunity which redevelopment of grounds presents to make better provision for disabled people. Many clubs already make provision for the disabled but this is by no means universal. Particular attention is needed to the provision of safe and adequately spacious viewing areas for wheelchair users, with a seat alongside for a companion, protected from the weather, accessible to toilet facilities designed specifically for the disabled, and easily reached from a car park (with reserved car spaces for Orange Badge holders) by means of ramps. The needs of other disabled people – those who have difficulty walking, the partially sighted, and those with impaired hearing – require special attention, for example by the provision of handrails, clear signposts, steps painted in bright colours, and the use of electronic scoreboards to supplement loudspeaker announcements, if these people are to be able to attend sporting events enjoyably and safely. I endorse the importance attached to these suggestions and I hope that the comprehensive improvements which I am proposing will include careful attention to them. Clubs should regard them as integral to their planning, not as an optional extra.

Conclusion

138. I hope in these two chapters I have made it clear that the years of patching up grounds, of having periodic disasters and narrowly avoiding many others by muddling through on a wing and a prayer must be over. A totally new approach across the whole field of football requires higher standards both in bricks and mortar and in human relationships.

PART II – SAFETY AT SPORTS GROUNDS

CHAPTER 3

THE FRAMEWORK

Minimum Standards of Safety

139. It is a truism that safety and crowd control are inter-dependent. If a crowd gets out of control safety will be in jeopardy. Measures to control the crowd, such as fencing, almost always have an impact on safety. Nevertheless, I shall seek to treat each separately. In this Part I shall deal with management and features of the ground affecting safety.

140. I have already stressed the need for football management to give higher priority to the safety and well-being of spectators. Clearly, the cost of safety measures and improvements can more easily be borne or raised by the successful clubs than by those struggling to keep going. But the safety of spectators invited to a ground cannot be left to depend upon the affluence of the club. There must be prescribed minimum requirements which have to be fulfilled at any ground if spectators are to be admitted there. The evidence of practice pre-Hillsborough and indeed post-Hillsborough, right up to December 1989, convinces me that the provisions presently in place, statutory and otherwise, have not been strong enough to enforce that basic level of safety.

Legislation for Safety

141. The principal instruments aimed at achieving a framework for safety are the Safety of Sports Grounds Act 1975 as amended by the Fire Safety and Safety of Places of Sport Act 1987 and the Home Office Guide to Safety at Sports Grounds (Green Guide).

142. The 1975 Act, as amended, requires a Safety Certificate to be issued by the local authority in respect of designated sports grounds. It is an offence (Section 12(1)(d)) to contravene any term or condition of the Certificate. Thus the requirements of the Certificate are mandatory but what those requirements should be is in the discretion of the local authority.

143. Section 2(1) of the 1975 Act provides:–

"A safety certificate shall contain such terms and conditions as the local authority consider necessary or expedient to secure reasonable safety at the stadium when it is in use for the specified activity or activities, and the terms and conditions may be such as to involve alterations or additions to the stadium."

144. Originally, certain obligatory terms had to be inserted in Safety Certificates. Section 2(2) provided:–

"Without prejudice to subsection (1) above, a safety certificate –

  (a) shall specify the maximum number of spectators to be admitted to the stadium;

  (b) may specify the maximum number to be admitted to different parts of it; and

  (c) shall include terms and conditions:–

    (i) as to the number, size and situation of entrances to and exits from the stadium or any part of it (including means of escape in case of fire or other emergency) and the means of access to any such entrances or exits;

    (ii) requiring those entrances, exits and means of access to be properly maintained and kept free from obstruction; and

    (iii) as to the number, strength and situation of any crush barriers."

However, when the Fire Safety and Safety of Places of Sport Act 1987 extended the application of the 1975 Act from sports stadia to all sports grounds, there was substituted for section 2(2), by section 19 of the 1987 Act, a new section 2(2) and a new section 15A giving power to the Secretary of State by order to lay down what terms and conditions a Safety Certificate shall include. No order has yet been made but guidance from the Home Office has recommended local authorities to approach their function under section 2(1) in accordance with the criteria in the superseded section 2(2). (See Home Office Circular 71/1987 dated 25 November 1987, Annex A, paragraph 6.)

145. So, presently, local authorities are not bound to include terms or conditions on any particular aspect of safety in the Certificate. In practice, they no doubt follow the Home Office guidance. They also take account of the Green Guide.

Green Guide

146. The latter, however, is by way of guidance only. It provides as follows:–

"6. Deviations from individual guidelines are possible without necessarily detracting from the overall safety of the ground. The variety of type, function and layout of sports grounds and the inter-relationship of the different parts of them means that a flexible approach should be maintained to take account of the particular circumstances at individual grounds".

Such flexibility is obviously highly desirable in relation to some aspects of the guidance. But flexibility can become degraded. Where a local authority has chosen to incorporate the criteria of the Green Guide into a Safety Certificate there has been scope for considerable deviation from provisions which ought to command standard adherence. Thus, for example, at Hillsborough where the Safety Certificate required compliance with certain Green Guide recommendations and a departure was shown to have occurred, the defence was that the Guide expressly provided for flexibility so that a deviation from its provisions was a matter of legitimate discretion.

147. In view of this and evidence I have received suggesting that the Green Guide may not be followed as closely as is desirable, I consider that when it is revised it needs to be given more effect. At present there is a risk of slackness developing in the absence of any mandatory provisions. There would appear to be two alternative courses open. It would be possible to make the terms of the Green Guide mandatory throughout. However, I think that this could be too rigid and in relation to some peripheral matters impractical. The other course is to make some of its provisions obligatory inclusions in the Safety Certificate. I prefer this.

148. **There are some requirements of such crucial importance to safety that it should be mandatory for Safety Certificates to specify them. I consider those specified in the original section 2(2) of the 1975 Act fall into this category. Moreover, so far as the original section 2(2)(b) is concerned "shall" should be substituted for "may".** This is critical to ensuring that no discrete area becomes overcrowded.

149. **Accordingly, I recommend that the Secretary of State exercise his specific powers under section 15A or his general powers under section 6(2) by order or regulation to achieve this.** In specifying the requirements in the Certificate, for a particular ground, the local authority should follow the Green Guide criteria; but once that is done and the appropriate figures and terms for that ground have been decided no room should be left for flexibility. By the stage when the local authority has specified the requirements in the Certificate, flexibility has been exhausted.

150. **Where a local authority incorporates any other provision of the Green Guide into the Safety Certificate it should make it clear whether that provision is to be complied with absolutely or with discretionary flexibility.** For example, paragraph 88 of the Green Guide provides that a ramp subject to heavy crowd flow should preferably not exceed a gradient of 1 in 10. Should a local authority require in a Safety Certificate that a club comply with a Green Guide recommendation as to gradients it should make clear whether it restricts gradients to a maximum of 1 in 10 or whether it leaves flexibility to the discretion of the club.

151. In putting the responsibility for the Safety Certificate upon the local authority, Parliament no doubt had two sound reasons; first, since all sports grounds differ in their layout and environs, local knowledge ought sensibly to be utilised in laying down and monitoring terms and conditions; secondly, a local body can respond quickly to any problem which may arise. Nevertheless, there are two aspects of such local administration which can cause problems.

(i) *The Advisory Group*

152. The issue, review and enforcement of Safety Certificates should be based upon efficient professional inspection and opinion and should be conducted in a businesslike manner. In Sheffield, the Safety Certificate procedure both for Hillsborough and for Sheffield United's ground at Bramall Lane was unsatisfactory as I indicated in paragraphs 150 to 158 of my Interim Report. I hope that this was exceptional. **It is important that there should be a safety team consisting of appropriate members of the local authority's own staff, representatives of the police, of the fire and ambulance services and of the building authority.** What name is given to this group does not in the end matter. At Sheffield it began by being called the Officer Working Party.

When Sheffield City Council took over from South Yorkshire County Council, the name was changed to the "Safety of Sports Grounds Advisory Group", or the Advisory Group for short. In my interim recommendations (Number 17) I said an Advisory Group should be set up. I had in mind the type of safety team already referred to. Apparently, in some quarters, it was thought that I was suggesting a second body called an Advisory Group to advise the safety team. This was not so. Also, in that recommendation, I suggested that representatives of the club and of a recognised supporters' club should be members of the Advisory Group. I have reconsidered this in the light of evidence and advice received. The responsibility for the Safety Certificate is exclusively that of the local authority. **I therefore think that the correct course is that representatives of the club and of a recognised supporters' organisation should be consulted,** since they may have relevant suggestions or criticisms to make, but they should not be full members of the team.

153. I repeat my recommendation that the Advisory Group's terms of reference should encompass all matters concerned with crowd safety and should require regular visits to the ground and attendance at matches. There should be a chairman from the local authority, and an effective procedure. Resolutions should be recorded and regular written reports should be required for consideration by the local authority.

(ii) *A Review Body*

154. The other disadvantage of Safety Certificates being issued locally is that different standards may be applied by different authorities even in practically identical situations. A safety team, or some very influential member of it, may be much stricter in one place than the comparable authority elsewhere. I have had complaints that since Hillsborough measures appropriate to a larger ground have been rigidly and inappropriately enforced at grounds with negligible attendance. Conversely, it is possible that too indulgent or lax an approach may be adopted or develop in a particular locality. Again, simply left to solve their own problems, there would be little opportunity for local authorities to learn from comparison with solutions adopted elsewhere. In these circumstances, it has been suggested that there should be a National Forum in which local authority teams could meet periodically to discuss and compare their procedures, and that there should be a national overseeing and inspecting body to monitor and review the consistent discharge by local authorities of their certificating duties. Having discussed this with local authority representatives both in England and in Scotland I am satisfied that two approaches are not necessary. **The better course is to have a National Inspectorate and Review Body. This is now provided for in the Football Spectators Act 1989 by section 13. It is there laid down that the Football Licensing Authority shall have the function of keeping under review the discharge by local authorities of their functions under the 1975 Act.** The FLA may, having consulted the local authority and certain local officers, require terms and conditions to be included in any Safety Certificate. The section empowers any inspector appointed by the FLA to make inspections and inquiry as necessary. The local authority may by notice be required to furnish the FLA with information regarding its discharge of its 1975 Act functions.

155. **I warmly welcome the appointment of a national body to conduct these inspecting and reviewing functions.** Assuming it successfully discharges those functions, the effect should be to improve the efficiency and consistency of practice with regard to the issue and review of Safety Certificates. This would be enhanced if the review body were to circulate, to all local authorities from time to time, advice based upon their experience of problems and solutions at various grounds. (See also Recommendation 16 of the report of the Technical Working Party at Appendix 3).

156. **Because the Football Spectators Act 1989 applies only to association football, the inspecting and reviewing role of the FLA would be exercisable only in relation to Safety Certificates at football grounds. Nevertheless, this remit of the FLA should be extended to cover all grounds designated under the 1975 Act and indeed all grounds requiring Safety Certificates or licences under Parts III and IV of the 1987 Act. Should Part I of the 1989 Act either not be implemented or be substantially delayed, the same functions should be given to another suitably constituted body to cover all sports grounds.**

157. It has been suggested that the Health and Safety Executive could fulfil this function if necessary or indeed that it could monitor spectator safety under the provisions of the Health and Safety at Work Etc Act 1974. However, its resources would need to be increased. Moreover, until now the Health and Safety Executive, being primarily concerned with the safety of employees pursuant to the 1974 Act, has not extended its surveillance to include spectators at football grounds. The Home Office evidence on this point is as follows:

"The Health and Safety at Work Act could also be used to enforce general spectator safety at sports grounds. Section 3 of the Act is wide ranging in that it places a duty on an employer to conduct his undertaking in such a way as to ensure, so far as is reasonably practicable, that persons not in his employment who may be affected thereby are not exposed to risks to their health or safety. A sports or other entertainment "undertaking" would fall within this category. However, it is the stated policy of the Health and Safety Commission that, as a general principle, they and the Executive wish to avoid duplication of enforcement with other authorities. The HSE would *not* therefore generally attempt to enforce the requirements of Section 3 of the 1974 Act when they overlap with duties imposed by other more specific legislation where other authorities have responsibility for policy and enforcement. The Safety of Sports Grounds Act 1975 represents more specific legislation and the Health and Safety Executive does not enforce Section 3 of the 1974 Act to secure the safety of spectators at sports grounds. This arrangement is agreed between the Health and Safety Executive and the Home Office."

CHAPTER 4

SUBSTANTIVE PROVISIONS

158. Having considered the framework for safety provided by the statutory provisions and the Green Guide, I must now deal with certain key substantive provisions.

Capacity

159. I accept the Technical Working Party's statement that "the safe allowable capacity of any viewing area whether seated or standing is the least of (i) its holding capacity, (ii) the number of persons who can leave through a normal exit system within a prescribed time at the end of an event, (iii) the number of persons who can leave through an emergency exit system within a prescribed time and (iv) the number of persons who can be admitted through the turnstiles serving that area within one hour." The "prescribed time" for normal exit is said in paragraph 230 of the Guide to be 8 minutes. The "prescribed time" for emergency exit is not definitively fixed in the Guide as it will vary from area to area. It will need to be determined by the local authority on advice from the Advisory Group and especially the fire service.

160. Subject to factors (ii), (iii) and (iv), where there is a properly designed seating area, capacity is simply determined by the number of seats. Increasingly, therefore, problems of maximum capacity will fade out as seating is phased in. But, as long as we have standing areas, grounds will be vulnerable to overcrowding and maximum limits must be set and achieved.

161. The Green Guide provides in paragraphs 221 and 222 for a maximum density of 54 persons per 10 sq metres assuming a terrace or viewing slope in good condition. For some reason, not easy to understand, the Guide also provides the lower figure of 27 persons per 10 sq metres when the slope or terrace "materially deviates from the recommended guidelines, so as to constitute a possible hazard to individuals closely packed". This might be taken to imply that whatever the hazards there is no need to reduce capacity below 27. In the heading to Chapter 16, the Green Guide emphasises that "account should be taken of the features of the individual ground, its configuration, general condition, use and any deviations from the Guide's provisions."

162. It became clear from evidence before me at both stages of this Inquiry that not only was the maximum of 54 per 10 sq metres grossly exceeded at Hillsborough; insufficient was being done generally to ensure either by counting or by informed assessment that the Green Guide criteria were observed. Accordingly, I reaffirmed the advice in the Guide and recommended that a reduction of 15% be made as an interim measure to improve the safety margin. The question now is what should be the final recommendation on this difficult subject.

163. I entirely agree with the Technical Working Party that there is no benefit to be gained from retaining the lower figure of 27 or any other minimum figure. Indeed, it could be a dangerous suggestion. **The scale of permissible density should be from 0 up to the maximum figure applicable only in good conditions.** I note the Technical Working Party's view that "*a uniformly distributed* density of 5.4/m^2 *should* be safe *in static conditions in full compliance with the Green Guide*". However, the words in italics are crucial to their view. It is one thing to place 54 docile people evenly in an area of 10 sq metres on a terrace and say they should be safe. It is quite another if they are excited, if they sway or surge to and fro, if one end of the area is a better viewing point than the other and if account is taken of possible incidents in the crowd eg a scuffle or a firework. Any of those factors can cause bunching; bunching can quickly become crushing.

164. Most clubs have responsibly applied the recommended 15% reduction. Some have jibbed at it; understandably, in view of its impact on revenue. On the other hand, as I have already observed, some Police Commanders expressed relief that numbers have been reduced. I must also point out that, even whilst the reduction has been in force, events have shown how easy it is for crushing to occur.

165. At the start of the 1989/90 season, on 19 August, Coventry were at home to Everton. There were complaints afterwards of congestion and crushing before the match outside the turnstiles and after the match as spectators pressed to get out.

166. Even more worrying was an incident on 9 December at Ayresome Park when Middlesbrough were at home to Leeds. I have not conducted a full inquiry into the incident having no remit to do so. But I have received a full report from the police. I have also viewed more than once a video film of what happened. It was horribly reminiscent of Hillsborough.

167. The following facts are clear. Leeds supporters had been allocated, as a standing area, a wedge-shaped pen "D" at the south east corner of the ground. It was flanked by a narrow sterile area on each side. There was a broad gangway running from top to bottom of pen "D". The perimeter fencing at the front of the pen was topped with spikes. There was not a single gate to the pitch. The only way out for those at the front was by a gate at each side into the sterile area and thence through another gate to the pitch. Those gates were closed during the match. The capacity of the pen in accordance with my interim recommendation was 2108. Leeds supporters were admitted to the pen, families with very young children being put at the front. The gangway was not kept clear. Some Leeds supporters managed to get tickets for the opposite home end of the ground causing apprehension of trouble. A number of them were taken out and moved into pen "D" from the pitch side. Other Leeds fans with tickets for the wrong end were also allowed into pen "D" from the back. Shortly after the match started, there was distress among those at the front of the pen. After two surges down part of the pen where there were no barriers from front to back, the police had to assist in getting spectators, especially children, out of the pen. This was done principally over the fencing although the side gates were opened and shut a number of times. In the event, 14 people had to be treated for minor injuries in the ambulance room. Five spectators, three of them children aged 10, 11 and 12, were taken to hospital with chest injuries, lacerations and bruising.

168. The local authority, the police and the club were clearly shocked by this incident and have taken prompt remedial action. Additional crush barriers are to be installed, additional gates are to be provided including one for pen D, the capacity of that pen is to be halved. Admission to all parts of the ground, save the visitors' section (pen D), is to be for members only to prevent away supporters buying tickets for the home end. Finally, there is to be a phased programme which will extend seating to all spectators by 1991/1992.

169. This incident and its aftermath prompt the query: does there have to be a disaster or near-disaster at each ground to trigger radical action? I hope not.

170. The permitted capacity of the pen was exceeded, although it is not clear to what extent. The police view is that it was only by about 60 persons. In a sense, the smaller the excess the more the point is made that danger can occur very quickly on a standing terrace even with moderate numbers. Some argue that reducing numbers and giving spectators more room simply enables a surge to gather greater momentum; that the tighter people are packed together the less the scope for surging or misbehaviour. This was the philosophy which allowed excessive numbers to be packed into pens prior to Hillsborough. The only sensible conclusion is that unless both numbers and terrace layouts are strictly controlled, there will always be a risk of crushing on a standing terrace. The combination of numbers, excitement and partisanship, even leaving aside misbehaviour, has a potential for danger.

171. Comparison with criteria adopted abroad is instructive. France and Belgium adopt the Green Guide figure of 5.4/m^2. But in Holland, the maximum standing capacity is 4/m^2. In Italy, the rule varies between municipalities. In Milan the figure is 2/m^2. In Rome it is 4/m^2. But in Italy little difference is recognised in principle between the figures permissible for standing and those for sitting.

172. Weighing all these factors I do not think it would be right to recommend a substantial departure from the effect of the 15% interim reduction. Now, rather than take a figure and deduct a percentage from it, **what is required is a specific figure for maximum standing density when terrace conditions are good by Green Guide criteria. I recommend that that figure should be 47 per 10 sq metres and I would substitute 47 for the figure of 54 in the Green Guide.** The effect is approximately a 13% rather than a 15% reduction from the former figure of 54. I wish to stress as forcefully as I can, however, that **this figure is a maximum and it is for the local authority acting on the recommendation of its Advisory Group to make necessary and realistic reductions from that figure in respect of any feature of the terrace which deviates significantly from Green Guide criteria or has any other significant shortcoming.**

Counting Them In

173. It is no use fixing a maximum capacity for a pen or enclosure unless there are reliable means of ensuring it is not exceeded. **I therefore repeat my recommendation that the number of spectators entering each self-contained pen or other standing area must be limited electronically, mechanically, by a ticketing arrangement, by counting or otherwise.** The best arrangement is one which makes all facilities for a single viewing area self-contained; access should be through turnstiles solely serving that area via a concourse doing likewise with its own toilets and refreshment points. This point has already been clearly made in paragraphs 101 and 206 of the Green Guide:–

"Each section should ideally be self-contained and should be serviced by its own entrance/exits, refreshment facilities and toilets . . ."

That way the numbers can be accurately recorded at the turnstiles on entry and no extra spectators can get into the area from elsewhere at half-time or after visiting common toilets or snack-bars.

174. Arrangements must be made to close off further access to each pen or area when maximum capacity is about to be reached and to close the turnstiles leading to the relevant area.

Gangways

175. The Green Guide, in paragraphs 97 to 99, makes recommendations as to gangways as follows:–

"Spectators should be discouraged from standing in lateral gangways because this disrupts free movement about the ground (or within sections of it). Also, spectators on the terrace steps behind the gangway may have their view obstructed, which will cause them to stretch and strain, and so generate dangerous pressures within the crowd. Spectators would be discouraged from standing in these gangways if they were sunk from 100mm to 200mm and if crush barriers were provided behind but not immediately in front of them.

Similarly, spectators should be discouraged from standing in radial gangways. These are relatively long and uncontrolled downward paths through terraces, and are difficult to keep clear, especially when sited in popular viewing areas, eg behind the goal area at a football ground. It is helpful to sink them 150mm to 200mm and to interrupt an otherwise continuously descending gangway by turns along, say, lateral gangways.

Where sinking gangways, lateral or radial, is not thought to be practical, their boundaries should be highlighted with paint and spectators advised by signs not to stand there. Stewards may be needed to enforce this instruction."

176. In my view these provisions need to be much tougher. **I agree with the Technical Working Party that gangways should be kept clear.** There is no point in having them, in calling them gangways and in excluding them from the area used to calculate capacity under paragraph 221 if spectators are allowed to stand in them. The whole point of crush barriers on terraces is to prevent unrestrained movement of large masses of fans from back to front down the terrace. It they are allowed to stand in the gangways where there are no barriers, such movement can occur without inhibition. The incident at Ayresome Park on 9 December 1989 involved just that. Two surges causing crushing against the fence came down the terrace unrestrained by barriers.

177. Whilst paragraph 98 of the Guide notes the difficulty of keeping radial gangways clear, it can be done. One way is to fix a radial rail on each side of the gangway and parallel to it, inhibiting lateral movement into the gangway from the standing areas. Another surprisingly effective method which I saw used successfully by Millwall is to put red and white tapes in the same position to indicate the gangway as a no-go area for standing.

178. **Gangways should be painted in a conspicuous colour** (yellow is used most commonly) **whether they are sunk or not. The Safety Certificate should require that no standing is allowed in gangways and that they be painted.**

Fencing

179. Perhaps the most emotive and disputed topic in this field is what should be done about perimeter fences. They were installed at many grounds to prevent pitch invasions during the 1970s. After Hillsborough there was a strong clamour to take them down. Some clubs did. Within weeks of Hillsborough, however, there were unruly incidents involving pitch invasions at more than one ground, as I noted in paragraph 308 of my Interim Report. I deferred making any interim recommendation involving structural alterations at the interim stage, confining myself to saying that gates to the pitch ought to be kept fully open.

180. Since then, whilst visiting grounds, I have seen a full range of practices from one extreme to the other. There is no consensus. At some grounds eg Highbury, there have never been perimeter fences. At others, like Anfield and White Hart Lane, there were fences but they have been taken down. At other grounds the fences vary in height and design. Some are fearsome high structures with florid arrangements of spikes, redolent of medieval weaponry. They look more suited to a prison than a sports ground. Coming down the scale, there are high fences with only vertical spikes and lower fences without spikes; fences of wire mesh and fences of strong metal; fences with a good provision of gates directly to the pitch, fences with only one gate per large pen (like Hillsborough), and some with no gate at all (as in pen D at Ayresome Park). Again, some clubs have left their gates to the pitch fully open as I recommended. Some have taken the gates out and left blank spaces;

some have opened the gates but put red and white tape across the gap; others have kept the gates open during the match, but closed them towards its conclusion to stop pitch invasions at the final whistle. Others again have kept the gates closed and bolted but manned individually. At Millwall's ground, an effective procedure is followed before each match whereby it is announced over the public address system that stewards will demonstrate the gates affording escape to the pitch. The stewards then do so in the manner of an air stewardess demonstrating emergency procedures. The gates are then closed to, but not locked.

181. This wide variety of practices is surprising. If a club were concerned only with its own supporters, divergence of practice would be readily understandable. Club A might say: "Our supporters can be trusted not to invade the pitch; so no fencing". Club B might say: "Some of our supporters have shown that given the chance they will invade the pitch, so we must have high fences to stop them". But all the clubs in any division, including clubs of type A and B, visit each other; so one has fans of club B, used to being caged in at home, being given the chance when visiting club A to invade the pitch. They do not seem to make a point of doing so with any frequency. However instances do occur, as I have mentioned; they are unpredictable and may happen at any time depending probably upon the occurrence of some incident thought to be provocative. When they occur, they can cause serious danger. There is risk of injury to players, to the referee and to the police, quite apart from the risk of injury through fighting between fans. It is true, as is often said, that so far no fatality has resulted from a pitch invasion, whereas 95 people died against a fence installed to prevent such invasion. But if fighting between fans starts on the pitch area, it is difficult to stop and injuries can be caused. At Selhurst Park on 13 May 1989, five police officers and 16 supporters required hospital treatment.

182. Since each club in a League division has to cope during the season with at least some of the supporters of all the other clubs in the division, the widely differing solutions to the fencing problem must be due to different attitudes rather than objectively different needs. The different attitudes taken by clubs or local authorities stem from the difficulty in balancing or deciding the priority of three crucial considerations:

  i.   Fences, especially high, spiked fences, are intimidating, ugly and demoralising.

  ii. Adequate measures must be taken to prevent pitch invasions for the reasons already given.

  iii. Whatever the measures taken to prevent pitch invasions, there must be adequate provision for escape in emergencies.

183. At some grounds, point ii. has been regarded as paramount so that i. has had to give way. At others, either point i. or, especially after Hillsborough, point iii. have carried greatest weight so as to remove or greatly reduce the fencing.

184. Is there any way of achieving a satisfactory balance of all three considerations? I believe so: that it is possible to have sufficient obstacles to pitch invasion without prison-type fences and also to provide for escape in emergency. I deal with the three considerations in turn.

i. High Spiked Fences

185. **I agree with the view that high, prison-type fences with spikes and overhanging sections should go.** The spectacle of these huge cage-like fences is inconsistent with a sports ground being for pleasure and recreation. Moreover, I believe such intimidatory fences have an adverse affect on both the morale and the behaviour of fans. They feel badly treated. Having to stand in a cage for your Saturday afternoon recreation inevitably causes resentment. Resentment often results in hostility to those controlling the match. A sour relationship develops and continues between the fans and those in authority, making the job of police and stewards much more difficult. Being inside the cage provokes some to hurl abuse or missiles at those outside, rival fans, players or police. The security of the fencing (in that the rival fans cannot penetrate it) encourages bravado to indulge in such activity. The spiked fences imply an expectation that trouble will or may occur. They also hamper a clear view of the game. To remove them would signal the advent of a new future for football and especially a new attitude from the authorities to the spectators. Accordingly, I consider that when perimeter fencing is used it should not exceed a prescribed maximum height and all spike arrangements and top sections angled inwards should go. This view is in accord with the recommendation of the Technical Working Party (Appendix 3 paragraph 20). But what should be the prescribed maximum height? That leads to consideration ii.

ii. Adequate Measures to Prevent Pitch Invasions

186. UEFA regulation B6 of 1988 requires as follows:–

"Protection of the playing field by means of

(a)   a fence of at least 2.2 metres in height or a moat or else

(b)   a barrier with adequate policing so as to make it impossible for spectators to enter the field of play.

Fences must have sufficient security gates opening towards the playing field and in the case of moats or a combination of moats and fences adequate other security passages should be provided".

187. Inquiries show that the figure of 2.2 metres was chosen simply by reference to the height of existing fencing at various grounds especially in West Germany and the need to choose a height of fence which would amount to "a real obstruction" to pitch invasion. As to the word "impossible" similar inquiries suggest that the intention was to leave it to the police commander to decide what resources he might need. Should a pitch invasion occur, UEFA would consider all the circumstances before deciding what if any action to take.

188. In my view a fence should be of sufficient height to be a serious obstacle to pitch invasion. It should provide sufficient obstruction to enable the police to take timely action should pitch invasion be attempted without being so high as seriously to interfere with vision or to give a feeling of imprisonment. Although I appreciate the UEFA regulation says "at least 2.2 metres", **these criteria lead me to recommend that perimeter fencing should be no higher than 2.2 metres. That measurement I take from ground level at the front of the terrace to the top of the fencing** ie the 2.2 metres may consist entirely of fencing or partly of wall and partly of fencing mounted on the wall. For example, at Ibrox Park the fencing is about 1.45 metres high but it is mounted on a wall and the total height of wall and fence is 2.2 metres.

189. In making this recommendation I am merely indicating a maximum height should perimeter fencing be used. I do not suggest there *must* be such fencing or indeed any fencing. Those clubs which presently have no perimeter fencing may well think it safe to continue that way. Others may emulate them. Still more may consider that they can dispense with fencing or bring it to a lower level than 2.2 metres in front of their family areas or their seated areas. As the seating areas increase it should progressively be found possible to achieve a corresponding reduction in fencing. These options, subject to the maximum height of 2.2 metres which I have indicated, should be left to the discretion of local authorities acting on the advice of their Advisory Group which will have consulted the club and supporters.

190. I should make clear that I have thus far referred only to perimeter fencing at the pitch side of viewing areas. Different considerations may well apply to the height of radial fencing used to segregate rival fans. The maximum height of such fences should be a matter for local decision and may depend for example on whether there are sterile areas between pens of rival fans; **but I still recommend that no spikes be used.**

191. Some may feel I am being naive or over-optimistic in recommending that fencing be brought down to a lower level. Hooligans may take advantage of this relaxation to have, literally, a field day. However, I draw attention to those grounds where fences have already been brought down to or below the level I recommend and others where there are none at all. If we wish to make progress, some initiative must surely be taken to stop the cycle of bad behaviour met with repression inducing worse behaviour.

192. Besides, there are other ways of deterring pitch invasions than by dauntingly fortified fences. One is to balance the lowering of the fences with a prohibition against going on to the pitch without reasonable excuse. I shall deal with that in the next chapter. The other is by alternative physical means.

Safety Corridors

193. One method has been adopted, so far successfully, at Anfield, Goodison Park and White Hart Lane. It involves reserving a safety corridor or dry moat between the front row of standing spectators and a perimeter fence or wall of moderate proportions. The two photographs Appendix 6 illustrate the Liverpool and Everton versions of it. The front few steps of the terrace are sacrificed as a viewing area and left as a sterile strip. Behind that area, the front row of crush barriers is filled in and made continuous with no gaps. The Everton version has no fence above the perimeter wall. At Anfield there is a low red rail fence. That arrangement does not absolutely prevent pitch invasion, but it inhibits it. Moreover, anyone or any group minded to get to the pitch has first to get over the front crush barrier, then cross the corridor, then get up the steps or over the wall onto the perimeter track. At White Hart Lane there is finally a line of advertising hoardings to be scaled. By that time the police should be able to intervene. At high-risk matches no doubt police could patrol the sterile area.

Moats

194. The safety corridor at these three grounds is not truly a dry moat. But I have seen examples both in Holland and Italy of a concrete dry moat providing a total obstacle to pitch invasion. At Utrecht, there is a deep broad moat; provision is made to enable spectators to descend into the moat and use it as a passageway for entrance and exit. A photograph is at Appendix 7. At the San Siro stadium in Milan, there is a similar moat at one side of the ground which will be extended all round. At present there is no provision for access to it or across it to the pitch but I was told in Rome that access to the pitch by bridges will have to be provided to accord with the Italian regulations.

195. To interpose a full scale moat of the Utrecht or Milan type between the spectators and the pitch requires considerable space. It is easier to provide it as an integral part of the design of a new stadium than to introduce it as a modification of an old one. At most UK grounds the space between pitch and spectators is very limited and to introduce a moat would involve a large loss of viewing area. Nevertheless, it is a solution worthy of consideration and especially so for a new stadium. Its advantage is that it effectively prevents pitch invasion without impeding vision or importing a prison atmosphere. A few rows back from it, you are not even aware of its existence. Its disadvantage, apart from the space it requires, is the difficulty of combining it with access to the pitch in emergencies.

iii Emergency Escape

196. Hillsborough showed conclusively that, if there are to be perimeter fences, there must be sufficient gates to permit escape to the pitch and they must be immediately available in an emergency. That lesson was reaffirmed by the recent incident at Ayresome Park. I know there is a school of thought opposed to access to the pitch in any circumstances, preferring that alternative evacuation routes should all be away from the pitch. Thus, at some grounds (Hillsborough was one) emergency plans did not require gates to the pitch or take any such existing gates into account in calculating the time required for alternative routes of evacuation. At Hillsborough, evacuation was to be via the central tunnel, or alternatively through the radial gates at the back of the terrace and round the ends of the west stand. But, if the emergency arises at the front of the terraces (as it did) those alternative routes cannot and did not afford timely relief. Presently, although emergency access to the pitch could readily be gained at both Anfield and Goodison Park, the plans do not rely on emergency evacuation in that direction. The tragic Bradford City disaster, in which fire swiftly engulfed a stand, would have caused much greater loss of life had there not been ready access to the pitch. It can no doubt be argued that inflammable stands with neglected underspaces should not recur, that with modern stands constructed of non-inflammable materials there should be no risk of another Bradford, and that if capacities and safety measures are observed no Hillsborough situation should recur. The solemn fact is that those two disasters did occur. One cannot predict what emergency may arise to make evacuation away from the pitch either wholly impractical or too slow.

197. The UEFA regulation cited above recognises that where there are fences access to the pitch should be preserved. **I agree with that view and recommend that emergency access to the pitch should be provided.**

198. How should this be done? There is no significant problem where there are either no fences or none higher than crush barrier level. At Anfield or Goodison Park, for example, it would not be difficult to get over the front crush barrier into the "dry moat" and thence to the pitch. That arrangement could be modified to include radial gangways at intervals running straight down to the "dry moat" through gaps in the front barrier. This would give even readier access. It must be for local judgement to balance the need for ready access to the pitch in emergencies with the need to deter such access otherwise.

199. The more difficult problem arises at grounds where fences of up to 2.2 metres are deemed necessary. **In such fences there must, in my view, be sufficient gates not less than 1.1 metre in width as approved by the Green Guide.** It is no use seeking to specify how many gates will be required by reference to the length of fencing at the front of a given pen or other enclosure. The length of the frontage is only one factor. Much will depend on the depth of the terrace and the numbers it is permitted to hold. I prefer, in concurrence with the Technical Working Party (Appendix 3 paragraph 22) to say that **the gates should be sufficient in number to enable the pen or other enclosure to be evacuated in the time required for any other emergency evacuation route. Such gates should be evenly spaced along the frontage of the pen to avoid congestion on exit.**

The Gates at Nimes

200. One solution to this problem is the system installed in the new stadium at Nimes which I visited together with the Assessors. There, the fence consists of a number of electrically operated panels which open as gates to the pitch, as shown in Appendix 8. There are six sections of the ground. The fencing in each section is governed by a trigger gate which may be operated electrically or manually. The post upon which it is

mounted has an electro-magnet which holds the mechanism inside the post in a position keeping the gate shut. When a button is pressed, the magnet is de-activated, the gate descends in its mounting and is free to swing towards the pitch. As it does so, it releases the next gate which is also mounted on a swivelling device within its post, operating by gravity to open the gate. This domino effect continues throughout the section. It can be arrested by someone leaning against one of the gates from the pitch side but how far anyone there could withstand substantial crowd pressure is doubtful. The trigger gate can be operated manually but this seemed to require considerable force. To shut the gate again seemed to require considerable force and a lifting motion. The gates are about nine inches higher than the front floor of the terrace, but there is no sump such as often exists in grounds in the UK. The system could be adapted to UK grounds but there are a number of factors upon which greater reassurance might be required. If the gates were fixed on top of a low wall such as that at Leppings Lane, there would be a danger of crushing in the sump or at least of broken limbs as people tried to get out. The system has been in operation at Nimes for only a few months and has not been severely tested to show that it would be effective under crowd pressure. Although a firm is licensed to market the system in 34 countries worldwide, our information is that so far they have been fitted only at Nimes and Toulon although one or two other French clubs are interested. In these circumstances the robustness of the fencing and the effects of English weather upon it are as yet unproved. At Nimes the system operates with a level walkway on the spectators' side of the fencing. Apart from a very small step, the pitch is at the same level. To achieve this arrangement would require considerable alteration to the layout of many UK grounds involving in particular raising the lower part of terraces to make them level with the pitch and with the bottom of the fencing.

Gates Unlocked

201. I made an interim recommendation to leave gates fully open when the pen or enclosure was occupied. This was for three stated reasons; first, to afford instant access to the pitch; secondly, to provide visual reassurance to fans after Hillsborough that there was an escape route and thirdly, to keep police and stewards alert to conditions inside the gateway. I also had in mind that the numbers and size of gates might at some grounds be inadequate and I was not making any recommendation for structural change at that stage. Along with reduced capacities, provision of sufficient gates and lower fences, I must now consider whether to keep or modify my recommendation to leave gates fully open. I know that some Police Commanders have been anxious that to do so is an invitation to pitch invasion; hence the practice at some grounds of closing the gates near the end of the game or keeping them shut but not locked. **I would still hope that gates would be left fully open wherever those in command feel this can safely be done. However, I recommend that whether they be fully open, partially open or closed they be kept unlocked throughout the period when the pen or enclosure is occupied.** They should thus be easily available for emergency exits and spectators should be confident of this.

202. **I repeat my interim recommendation that all gates in radial and perimeter fences of pens or other self-contained areas should be painted in a different colour from the rest of the fences and marked "Emergency Exit".**

Authorising Access to the Pitch

203. Interim recommendation number 9 provided as follows:–

" * 9. There should be in respect of each gate in a perimeter fence (or group of gates if they are close together) a police officer authorised to decide whether or not to allow spectators through a gate to relieve overcrowding . . ."

Despite the much greater alertness to the possibility of an emergency which now exists, following Hillsborough, I still believe it necessary to make a recommendation to ensure that proper provision is made for swift action to authorise the opening of gates in the event of an emergency. However, it has been drawn to my attention that strict observance of this interim recommendation verges on the absurd where a pen contains only a handful of spectators. Moreover, to be bound to provide a police officer at each gate or group of gates in all circumstances involves a heavy commitment of police manpower which would be even heavier with an increase in the number of gates. **Accordingly, I have decided to recommend that although each gate should be manned when the enclosure is occupied, whether such manning should be by a police officer or by a steward is for the Police Commander to decide. In either event plans should ensure that the police can authorise access through gates to the pitch immediately in the event of an emergency.**

Monitoring Crowd Density

204. It is convenient to mention a modification I think sensible regarding interim recommendation 5. That provided:–

" * 5. At each match, there should be on the perimeter track, for each self-contained pen or other terraced area, a steward (if the club is monitoring that area) or a police officer (if the police are monitoring it) whose sole duty is to check crowd conditions in that area for possible overcrowding or distress throughout the period the area is occupied by spectators. Whoever is so appointed should be in addition to any other steward or police presence. He should have ready access to the police officer authorised under Recommendation 9 below, and by radio to the control room."

I repeat that recommendation (with a slight change of wording to achieve clarity) but qualify it to avoid absurdity when numbers are small. The recommendation need not be applied to any self-contained pen or other standing area where the spectators present, or reasonably to be expected, during a particular match do not exceed one third of the area's maximum permitted capacity, or 2,000, whichever is the lower.

Cutting Equipment

205. In the immediate aftermath of Hillsborough, I recommended that suitable and sufficient cutting equipment should be provided to enable spectators to be released from behind perimeter fencing. Assuming the recommended maximum capacities are observed, that fences are lowered, that sufficient gates are provided and left unlocked, cutting equipment should not be necessary. Something in these provisions would have to go badly wrong for such equipment to be required. **Nevertheless, I recommend that the equipment should be maintained in case of some unforeseen emergency.**

Functions of Police and Stewards

206. Which functions should be discharged by the police and which by the club's stewards is one of the most vexed questions. To describe the background to the argument I can do no better than repeat what I said in my Interim Report at pages 28 and 29.

"Who should Monitor the Terraces?

161. Should it be the host club via its stewards? Should it be both? Or should it be by arrangement, depending upon the ground or section of the ground in question?

162. In principle, a football club which invites the public to a match on its premises for reward is responsible for securing safety at that event. The Green Guide (1986) provides:

"23. The safety of the public inside the ground is the responsibility of those who stage the event and administer the ground in which it is held, *ie* the "management". This responsibility applies in both normal and emergency situations . . .

195. . . . there are five basic duties which stewards are called upon to carry out. These are:

(a) controlling or directing members of the public who are entering or leaving the ground, to help achieve an even flow of people to the viewing areas and safe dispersal of spectators on the terraces or viewing slopes;

(b) patrolling the ground to deal with any emergencies, *eg* raising alarms or extinguishing fires;

(c) manning entrances, exits and other strategic points, especially exit doors and gates which are continuously open whilst the ground is in use;

(d) assisting police as appropriate or as requested with crowd control; and

(e) undertaking specific duties in an emergency."

The Interim Popplewell Report

163. There was considerable controversy in the course of the public inquiry held by Mr Justice Popplewell in 1985 as to the responsibility of the club and the police. In paragraph 3.6 of his interim report, Mr Justice Popplewell quoted from a report produced for the Minister of Housing and Local Government in 1969 as follows:–

"The responsibility for controlling crowd behaviour is divided between the police and the club operating the ground. The broad line of division being that police are responsible for movement of spectators in public thoroughfares and from public thoroughfares into the ground, while the club is responsible for the control of spectators once they are on the club's premises . . ."

Mr Justice Popplewell said he did not quarrel with that view and went on to observe that in practice the police have to take charge and be responsible for controlling crowd behaviour. He then said (paragraph 3.8):

"It follows, therefore, that as a matter of practice, while the physical safety of the building and the maintenance and good housekeeping of the ground must always be the responsibility of the club, the police have to take the *de facto* responsibility of organising the crowd, with all that entails, during the game..."

Mr Justice Popplewell went on to instance evacuation of the ground as a procedure in which only the police could bear the responsibility of supervising the organisation of the crowd.

The Final Popplewell Report

164. He harked back to this subject in chapter 4 of his Final Report. There, he came down more firmly in favour of holding the club responsible for crowd safety. At paragraph 4.13 he said "Because, as a matter of practice, police officers have regularly attended in large numbers at football grounds, it has somehow been assumed by the clubs that the responsibility for control of what goes on inside the ground has passed from them to the police. A police presence is there to assist in the enforcement of law and order. Those responsible for organising a private function, however, have the primary and continuing obligation and responsibility to ensure reasonable safety for those who are invited on to their premises." Mr Justice Popplewell ended that section as follows: "It cannot be too strongly emphasised that it is upon the club, or the occupier of the ground who is putting on the function, that the primary and continuing obligation rests."

165. There remains, however, the question whether there are some grounds or parts of grounds where the club may need to rely upon the police (whom they pay to attend) to control filling of pens and monitoring them for overcrowding. In other words, whilst the duty in law to ensure safety rests upon the club, they may need, and by agreement be entitled, to employ the police to act as their agents in certain circumstances. This very difficult and grey area as to club and police responsibility will need to be reviewed in greater depth at stage two of this Inquiry."

Since Hillsborough was concerned with a disaster on the terraces, I headed that passage "Who should monitor the terraces?". But the wider question is: who should control the entry of spectators, their placing and movement whilst in the ground and their exit from it? It is undisputed that the club, as a matter of law, has a duty to take reasonable care for the safety of the spectators invited to its premises. There have, however, been two practical difficulties about the club, rather than the police, being *de facto* in charge.

207. First, the club discharges its duty through stewards. They are part-time employees or assistants whose duties are confined to match days. Many of them are seasoned supporters of the club and some tend to be elderly: others are keen young supporters. Due either to age or youth, many therefore lack the physique to cope with awkward customers. They are usually not well paid, part of their "remuneration" (indeed all of it at some clubs) consisting of the opportunity to see the game. As the submission from the Association of Chief Police Officers of England, Wales and Northern Ireland (ACPO) puts it:

"(Stewards) are at best casual workers (usually working one day in two weeks), they are probably not people who have a supervisory role in ordinary life and are not always equipped or used to giving directions or facing obstruction. Many are retired people and pay is not so attractive as to guarantee commitment."

Whilst there are exceptions, I have frequently been told that the stewards presently employed at many clubs are of limited capacity and reliability.

208. Secondly, there has to be a police presence at a match to maintain law and order. Police are trained to give and enforce instructions. This, together with the uniform they wear and the respect for and fear of the law which the majority of spectators have, gives the police far more authority than stewards. Moreover, if trouble arises, whether from misbehaviour or from any other cause, the police will inevitably be drawn into assuming control. They have all the means to do so at their disposal – the control room, the CCTV, the planned deployment of serials of officers round the ground, a communications system to co-ordinate them and reserves on call. The submission from ACPO suggests that in these circumstances, and to avoid confusion, the police ought to accept prime responsibility for controlling the crowd. I quote two passages from their argument:

"It may be that the ambiguous position of the police is part of the problem – that is acknowledging the club's responsibility for safety on the one hand, whilst routinely assuming all those tasks of stewarding which the stewards cannot do, either because of the truculence of supporters or the limited talents of the stewards themselves, on the other. It has to be said that the present lack of clarity in these arrangements can lead to something of a 'dog's dinner'. In some clubs the police actively control the stewards, in others the stewards are quite independent and, despite some improvements, standards of stewarding vary considerably with many being too old or simply unreliable...

... It may be better to acknowledge that if trouble is anticipated or if crowd control is going to test the ground capacities then, in the interests of public safety, police should take control over the stewards through their supervisory chain".

"As to the question of 'responsibility', the matter of civil liability should not cause us to resile from our decisions if they are necessary. Dual responsibility for safety is a recipe for confusion. The police are always going to seize the initiative in a crisis; crowd control is always going to be inextricably linked to criminal hooliganism: the police are never going to accept direction from stewards; stewarding will never (at least not in the foreseeable future) be able to cope without some law enforcement backup; and finally police do 'own' most of the means of control. In these circumstances the police must accept a leading role and, despite the requirements and civil liabilities of football clubs, themselves take on supervision of the overall conduct of events wherever crowd safety is an issue."

209. The question is one of balance. Carrying delegation to its ultimate, clubs could lean back and leave it to the police to take over the management of spectators from street to terraces and back again, with stewards performing a minimal role. This would involve a very heavy police commitment and indeed the commitment at present is very substantial. As already indicated, some 5,000 officers or more are deployed every Saturday at football matches.

Costs of Police and Stewards

210. The temptation to the clubs to leave it all to the police is stronger if they are not required to make realistic payment for police services. No charge is made for officers outside the ground since maintaining law and order in the streets is a normal public function of the police. At the present time, the practice as to recovering costs of policing inside the grounds from clubs varies greatly from place to place, different formulae being used. In some areas, the charge made is the actual cost of the officers attending in the ground. At others, it is made on a sliding scale dependent on whether the match is category A (high-risk) B or C. At others it is dependent on the size of the crowd attending. At some, it appears to be entirely arbitrary and at one ground it is said to be nil. **In my view a more consistent and businesslike approach should be made to such charges.** If clubs were to find it more economical to recruit efficient stewards than to delegate duties to the police, there could be a significant reduction in the number of police deployed at football grounds to the benefit of the community at large. If this is to happen, **stewards must be fit, active and robust. I would suggest they should be between the ages of 18 and 55. They must also be fully trained.** Some clubs presently have efficient stewards whom they recruit individually and train fully with the assistance of the police. Others hire security firms to bring in a well-trained team of stewards.

Division of Functions

211. There are clearly many aspects of crowd control and management which are capable of being carried out by efficient stewards. Manning gates, directing spectators to the correct areas and to their seats, keeping gangways clear, monitoring the density of packing in pens or enclosures – indeed, the duties specified in paragraph 195 of the Green Guide, as already quoted. At most grounds, and in most parts of each ground, these duties ought to be capable of being performed by properly trained stewards. Where that is so, clubs should require stewards to perform the duties and should not take the option of leaving all to the police.

212. However, I accept that there may well be particular areas of a ground, perhaps on visitors' terraces and particularly at high-risk matches, which call for the greater authority and resilience of the police. What the division of functions should be must be a matter for local decision and in the last resort for the Police Commander to determine.

Written Statement of Intent

213. **I therefore repeat my recommendation that there should be a written document setting out the respective functions of club and police for crowd safety and control "and in particular for the filling of each self-contained pen or other terraced area and the monitoring of spectators in each such pen or area to avoid**

overcrowding." (Interim recommendation 4). The aim should be for the club through its stewards to perform all those functions of controlling spectators of which they are capable having regard to the quality of the stewards, the layout of the ground and the nature of the match. Where they are not able to discharge any such function the police should perform it. As the proportion of seating at grounds increases, control by stewards should become the norm.

214. In making interim recommendation 4, I used the phrase "written agreement". This led to anxiety that what was required was a binding legal contract which would deprive the police of any flexibility in response to circumstances of the day. My intention was not to shackle either party by a binding contract; it was simply to have a document setting out how functions were to be divided so that no misunderstanding could arise whereby one party thought the other had undertaken some duty and vice versa. **I am content that the document be referred to simply as a "statement of intent",** so that it can be subject to alteration without breach of contract should circumstances so demand.

Police Commanders

215. The ultimate control at any match must be that of the Police Commander. He has authority to decide how many officers he needs and to deploy them in and outside the ground. He has, if necessary, to take such decisions as to postpone kick-off, to stop the match, to evacuate the ground or any area of it. Police Commanders tend to remain in post for lengthy periods. They thus acquire skill, experience and special knowledge of the problems at their particular ground. However, there must come a time for change. It is then essential for the new Commander to have adequate time and training to acquaint himself with his functions and the problems of policing peculiar to the ground. **Training for such functions should be the subject of a specific course to be attended by senior officers presently acting as Police Commanders and those in line to do so. Such a course would give induction training in the basic strategy of policing football matches** and would also give opportunity for the pooling of experience and the solution of common problems.

Rate of Admission

216. An important causative factor at Hillsborough was the congestion which built up outside the turnstiles in the last 20 minutes before kick-off. Twenty-three turnstiles were required to admit 24,256 spectators; only seven turnstiles were available to admit the 10,100 with tickets for the west terraces. Much was made in evidence of the late arrival of the Liverpool fans. However, further evidence at stage two of the Inquiry suggests that the late arrival of large numbers is a common feature at many grounds. Apart from those wishing to drink as long as possible (whom I consider in chapter 6) there are many who do not care to stand or even sit for a long period in addition to the 90 minutes of the match. Moreover, at all-ticket matches or to those with tickets in seated areas, there seems little reason to arrive early since places are assured. The absence of any attractive pre-match entertainment is a further disincentive to early arrival. Whilst measures should be taken to encourage earlier entry to the ground, it is essential that turnstiles or other entrances can cope safely and efficiently with spectators as and when they arrive. To do this requires sufficient turnstiles or other entrances to admit, if necessary, a large late influx without dangerous congestion. That involves assessing the rate of flow through turnstiles or gates and the time within which they should be capable of admitting all the spectators they are intended to serve.

217. I accept the view of the Technical Working Party that the Green Guide figure of 750 persons per hour is too optimistic a turnstile flow-rate. It may be achieved or even bettered in ideal conditions. But as soon as there is a build-up, the flow-rate will diminish. There are also delays caused by those with no tickets, those with wrong tickets or other problems. **I accept the recommendation that 660 should be the maximum notional rate. The Green Guide should be amended accordingly.**

218. **I repeat my interim recommendation that the turnstiles serving a discrete area should be capable of admitting its holding capacity within one hour.** Unless this can be done, there will be a risk of serious congestion in the last half or quarter of an hour. **If it cannot be done, the permitted capacity of the area must be reduced accordingly. This recommendation relates to one of the crucial matters contained in the original section 2(2)(c)(i) of the 1975 Act and should therefore be a requirement of the Safety Certificate.**

Communications

219. The efficient deployment and co-ordination of police and stewards depend upon effective systems of communication. Radio systems are susceptible to two problems; excessive air traffic on the channels in use and the volume of noise from the crowd.

220. If large numbers of officers are issued with radios and are all entitled to use the same channel, confusion may result should a major incident occur. In such an event, many officers may wish to speak simultaneously. Especially if the channel is used on "talk-through" (whereby all officers including those in control give and receive messages without priority) the Commander in the police room may be unable effectively to issue orders. Again, if the level of crowd noise is high, as it often is, an officer on the perimeter track may have great difficulty in hearing messages. Although ear pieces are of some assistance, they are not totally successful in excluding crowd noise and are not usually issued to every officer carrying a radio.

221. Mr Justice Popplewell in his Interim Report recommended that "early attention should be given by the Home Office Directorate of Telecommunications to consider the practicality of producing a more suitable personal radio for the police". In his Final Report, he returned to the subject at paragraphs 4.102-104. By that time, he reported that "a detailed study is being commissioned by the Home Office Directorate of Telecommunications into the problem of personal radios".

222. The Directorate produced an upgraded specification. As a result, supplies of two new models have been made available. They are the Philips PFX and the Motorola MT600E. These radios have greater range and clarity than those previously used. They also give access to many more channels. To take advantage of this, the police have been allocated eight additional UHF frequencies.

223. Police Commanders have told me that, in addition to any other channel or channels in use, **there should always be a command channel reserved solely for the Police Commander to communicate with his senior officers round the ground.** This is of the first importance since it enables the Commander to use the information coming to him in the control room to deploy his forces promptly and effectively at any part of the ground without radio interruption. **I recommend this should be done.**

224. As suggested by the Technical Working Party, **I repeat the recommendations I made in my Interim Report as to communications, with one exception.** A sentence in one recommendation suggested that "consideration should also be given to the use by police officers of a simple code of hand signals to indicate to the control room the existence of certain emergencies or requirements." **I am persuaded by evidence from the police that the use of hand signals could create a risk of confusion and I do not therefore repeat that suggestion.**

Other Topics in the Green Guide

225. I have in this chapter considered specifically a number of key safety factors covered by the Green Guide. I have suggested respects in which the Guide should be strengthened or amended. In addition to those topics, **the Technical Working Party considered a number of further aspects of safety – crush barriers, stands, ingress and egress, stairways and ramps, inspections and testing, fire safety, emergency power and disabled spectators. I accept and adopt the Technical Working Party's Report and recommendations on those matters** (Appendix 3). Without repeating them in this text, I add only a few additional comments.

226. **As to crush barriers,** paragraphs 25 to 28 of their report recommend a simpler and clearer test procedure than that in the current Guide. In particular, **the values to be achieved by way of percentage recovery after the required loading test will depend upon the material from which the barrier is constructed eg concrete, steel or wrought iron. When the Guide is revised, acceptable values for various materials should be specified.**

227. The Green Guide does, in paragraph 6 of Annex C, refer to the possibility of doubts arising as to the safety of a barrier "for any reason (including such matters as cracking of the terracing or distortion of connections)". It does not, however, presently make any special mention of the need to inspect crush barriers for possible corrosion. The evidence from the Health and Safety Executive after their inspection of barriers at Hillsborough suggests that corrosion is a serious threat to the safety of metal barriers. **When the Green Guide is revised, the need to inspect for possible corrosion should be specifically mentioned and emphasised.**

Co-ordination of Emergency Services

228. It is vital that adequate provision should be made for possible emergencies arising from fire or accident and from illness or injuries however caused. **I repeat the recommendations I made in my Interim Report regarding co-ordination of the emergency services.** In addition, although it is mentioned in paragraph 176 of the Green Guide, I emphasise that "joint consultation between management, police, fire, ambulance and other emergency services should take place in order to produce agreed plans of action for all foreseeable types of emergency." Such plans should include, for example, contingency arrangements for admissions to particular hospitals in the event of a number of casualties and consideration of possible casualty clearing areas at the sports ground. **Lines of communication, whether by telephone or by radio, from the police control room to the local headquarters of all emergency services should be maintained at all times so that emergency calls can be made instantly.**

First Aid, Medical Facilities and Ambulances

229. The scale of available medical facilities has been the subject of controversy. After Hillsborough, there were complaints of insufficient basic equipment such as stretchers. I repeat what I said in my Interim Report at paragraphs 298 and 299:–

"298. It would be unreasonable to expect, at any sports stadium, medical facilities capable of dealing with a major disaster such as occurred. To have in advance at the ground, oxygen, resuscitators, stretchers, other equipment and medical staff sufficient to deal with over 100 casualties is not practicable.

299. What is required is a basic level of provision for first aid, for professional medical attention and for ambulance attendance, together with a system of co-ordination with the emergency services which will bring them to the scene swiftly in whatever numbers are required. What will amount to an appropriate basic provision for the future *eg* the equipment in a first aid room, requires expert evaluation and advice".

230. **The Scottish ambulance service has developed a "major incident equipment vehicle" designed and equipped to deal with up to 50 casualties. It is packed with 50 stretchers, blankets, and medical supplies and is in effect a travelling storehouse for such equipment. A vehicle of that type is deployed in addition to other ambulance attendance at matches with crowds over 25,000. This provision goes a long way towards meeting the criticism raised after Hillsborough and I recommend that it be adopted elsewhere.**

231. **I repeat the Interim Recommendations I made under this heading subject to two variations.** First, it has been sensibly urged that it is unreasonable to require a medical practitioner to be present throughout a match where attendance is very small. At such a match it is suggested that to have a medical practitioner on call would be sufficient. **I agree with this and recommend that the full-time presence of a doctor should not be required where there is no reasonable expectation of more than 2,000 spectators attending.**

232. Secondly, some clubs have told me that they can secure private ambulance services more economically than those from the appropriate ambulance authority. They accordingly wish to have freedom to choose. **I modify my Interim Recommendation in deference to this argument by requiring at least one fully equipped ambulance from, *or approved by*, the appropriate ambulance authority should be in attendance at all matches with an expected crowd of 5,000 or more.**

Status of the Green Guide

233. I have recommended that some safety factors covered by the Guide should be made mandatory requirements in Safety Certificates. Those apart, I consider the Guide should remain a non-mandatory set of guidelines. Sports grounds vary greatly in their layout and fixtures. It must be open to a local authority to judge the propriety of deviating in some respect from the Green Guide recommendations at a particular ground. However, I agree with the Technical Working Party that where there is a departure from a specific recommendation of the Guide, the local authority should be aware of it and should be satisfied that such departure is justified for good reason.

Revision of the Green Guide

234. Neither I nor the Technical Working Party have sought to revise or redraft the specific wording of the Guide. We have simply indicated where and to what effect it should be altered. Detailed consideration of the revision must be for a suitably qualified body to be set up by the Home Office for the purpose. The Technical Working Party, in addition to their report, have prepared detailed supplementary notes on some aspects of the Guide which will be available and I am sure useful to those revising it. **Accordingly, I recommend that the Home Office set up a body to revise the Green Guide as a matter of urgency.**

Sports Grounds Within Part III of the Fire Safety and Safety of Places of Sport Act 1987

235. This Part of the 1987 Act applies in relation to a sports ground which is not a designated sports ground but which provides covered accommodation in stands for spectators. A Safety Certificate is required where such a stand provides covered accommodation for 500 or more spectators. By section 27(1) the Safety Certificate:–

"shall contain such terms and conditions as the local authority consider necessary or expedient to secure reasonable safety in the stand when it is in use for viewing the specified activity or activities at the ground, and the terms and conditions may be such as to involve alterations or additions to the stand or any installations in or serving the stand."

236. These provisions apply to a variety of sports such as tennis, golf, horseracing, greyhound racing or motor racing.

237. I have received a number of complaints that local authorities, perhaps in response to Hillsborough, have sought to apply the full rigour of my Interim Recommendations to sports grounds requiring a Safety Certificate under these provisions, not being designated sports grounds under the 1975 Act. On occasion this has been done without regard to the Green Guide or to Home Office guidance. Examples given are requirements in relation to greyhound stadia regarding the presence of a medical practitioner, the size of a first aid room, and capacity of parts of the stadium other than the covered stand itself.

238. The Green Guide provides at paragraph 5 as follows:–

"The Guide is intended to cover grounds where sporting events of all kinds are held and where the gathering of large crowds is likely to present a safety problem. However, much of the guidance has particular application to football stadia and this should be borne in mind when applying the Guide to grounds used for other sports and modifications may prove necessary, because the measures to meet problems of stadia used for association football may not always be necessary at other grounds used for other types of sports. For example, if a ground has no terraced or sloped viewing areas, crush barrier requirements are unlikely to be of concern".

A similar approach is appropriate in relation to my Final Recommendations. They are essentially directed towards designated sports grounds. Many are relevant to other sports grounds but will need to be applied with due regard to the different circumstances at those other sports grounds.

239. One appropriate function of the inspecting and reviewing body, which I propose should cover all certificating and licensing of sports grounds, would be to ensure that recommendations in the Green Guide and those made in this Report are applied sensibly across the varied range of sports grounds.

Sports Grounds Within Part IV of the Fire Safety and Safety of Places of Sport Act 1987

240. This Part of the 1987 Act relates to indoor sports licences. It introduced amendments to the London Government Act 1963 and the Local Government (Miscellaneous Provisions) Act 1982 requiring a licence to be granted by the relevant local authority where premises are to be used for "any entertainment which consists of any sporting event to which the public are invited as spectators" (a "sports entertainment").

241. Under this legislation, the relevant local authority:–

"may grant to any applicant, and from time to time renew, a licence for the use of any premises specified in it for any sports entertainment on such terms and conditions and subject to such restrictions as may be so specified".

242. I have received evidence from a number of bodies complaining that the procedure followed in pursuance of these provisions often requires different applications to be made by different applicants for different "sports entertainments" at the same premises. Apart from the expenditure of time and effort, such multiple applications tend to be expensive to amateur sports organisations which are often impecunious. The suggestion is made that a procedure should be available whereby a licence for a range of "sports entertainments" at the same premises could be obtained by a single operator periodically. This matter merits review by the appropriate authorities.

PART III – CROWD CONTROL AND HOOLIGANISM

CHAPTER 5

POLICE PLANNING AND CONTROL

243. The role of the police is crucial to crowd control. In my findings as to what happened at Hillsborough and why, I criticised the police operation on the day and especially some senior officers. I did, however, recognise that the South Yorkshire Police had a good record, that day apart, for handling difficult crowd problems successfully. I also commended many junior officers for their efforts to rescue and assist those crushed or trapped at Hillsborough.

244. I should like here to pay tribute to police forces generally for their invaluable work in maintaining order at sports events and especially in and outside football stadia, Saturday after Saturday. Without them, sports events would be chaotic and indeed many could not be permitted to take place. Their service is often thankless and not infrequently they are subjected to abuse and worse from those they are there to serve.

245. They would be superhuman if on occasions they did not react, at any rate verbally, to the stress and provocation they have to endure. This leads many fans to feel the police are against them. Moreover, it is often difficult in the confusion of a crowded scene for firm police action against miscreants not to impinge also, or focus by mistake, on the innocent. The latter then feel aggrieved and others become aggrieved on their behalf.

246. It is therefore vital that police discipline and self-control be of the highest standard and that friendly relations with supporters are cultivated. I know and have myself seen that this is achieved at many grounds. But there are reports that, at some places, some police treat supporters, especially away supporters, with a measure of contempt. When this happens it unfortunately sours the attitude of the supporters towards all police.

247. Accordingly, Police Commanders should in their briefings stress the need to balance firm control with good humour and patience.

248. **As to the planning of police operations and the techniques to be considered, I repeat my interim recommendations (numbers 6 and 26 to 30) which are now recommendations 16, 44 to 46, 49 and 51.**

Police Control Room

249. **It is essential to efficient police operations that their control room inside the ground should be well placed, of sufficient size and well equipped.** A number I have seen have been very good. Some are too small, however. **There should be room for at least the Commander, his deputy and enough officers to man the radios, telephones and CCTV screens. The room should leave space for others who may need from time to time to visit the room eg other senior officers, club management or a member of the emergency services. The room should command a good view of the whole pitch and of the spectator areas surrounding it. It should where necessary be sound-proofed against excessive crowd noise.** Failure to provide the police with a satisfactory control room is misguided thrift.

CHAPTER 6

ALCOHOL

250. There can be no doubt that excessive drinking by fans significantly aggravates problems of crowd control. Because alcohol tends to remove inhibitions and self control, those who have drunk too much may become aggressive and even violent especially when provoked. Short of this, however, alcohol can make fans resistant to sensible and reasonable instructions, more impatient and less considerate of others. All of this increases the problems for police and stewards in managing large numbers which is difficult enough even with co-operation.

Legislation

251. In Scotland, serious crowd misbehaviour, much of it drink-related, led to the appointment in 1976 of the Working Group chaired by Mr Frank McElhone MP. The recommendations of his report were followed in the Criminal Justice (Scotland) Act 1980 which made it an offence to be in, or to attempt to enter, a designated ground while in possession of alcohol or to be in, or to attempt to enter, the ground whilst drunk. It also banned the possession of alcoholic liquor on public service vehicles carrying passengers to or from a designated sporting event and by amendment this ban was extended to vehicles adapted to carry nine or more passengers.

252. I am in no doubt after discussions with senior Scottish police officers that this measure has greatly reduced the problem of misbehaviour at Scottish football grounds. Sectarian violence still has to be contained, especially at Rangers and Celtic matches. There is still trouble from the "new hooligan" groups, known in Scotland as "casuals". But much of the misbehaviour of groups II and III in the Popplewell classification has abated due to the firm enforcement of the 1980 Act by the Scottish police.

253. In England and Wales this lead was followed in the Sporting Events (Control of Alcohol etc) Act 1985 which made similar provisions.

254. There is, however, an important difference between the Scottish provisions and those applying in England and Wales. In Scotland, the ban on alcohol is absolute. No sales of alcoholic drink are permitted in the ground. In England and Wales, section 3 of the 1985 Act permits Licensing Justices to grant exemption from the ban on sales in the ground. This is subject to alcohol not being sold or consumed at any part of the ground from which the sporting event may be directly viewed and to other conditions imposed by the Justices. It is open to the Justices to revoke or vary an order and the police have power to shut down the sale of alcohol at a particular event if they consider it would be detrimental to orderly conduct or safety.

Alcohol Sales in Grounds?

255. It is against this background that I must consider the submission of the FA and others that sale of alcoholic drink in football grounds should be generally permitted without need to obtain an exemption order. The argument is that the ban on such sales does not prevent fans from drinking. It merely drives them to drink in public houses until a short time before the match. They then arrive late, often inebriated and truculent, thereby causing congestion and other problems at entrances. Far better, it is said, to make alcoholic drink available at the ground so as to bring them in earlier. Since service of drink inside the ground is slow and selling points are crowded it is argued that the visitor will be lucky to buy more than one round. He is therefore unlikely to become drunk from drinking inside the ground.

256. Ideally I accept that people attending a football match should be able to buy refreshments including alcoholic drink just as they can at the theatre or other places of entertainment. I hope, in halcyon days ahead, a better atmosphere at football grounds may justify bans being relaxed. I do not, however, think the present time is ripe for such relaxation.

257. I have mentioned the great improvement of crowd behaviour in Scotland where the ban is absolute and has been in force now for nearly 10 years. No doubt other factors such as increased seating have played their part in this. The improvement has been recognised by the Government, and is the main reason why the Football Spectators Act 1989 has not been applied to Scotland. Thus Mr Moynihan, the Minister for Sport, said on the Third Day of the Committee Stage (Official Report, column 83):

"There has been a marked improvement in the behaviour of football crowds in Scotland, which is accepted by all parties and the Scottish Football Association. The Scottish Office is monitoring developments closely and . . . it does not believe that it is necessary to legislate for a national membership scheme in Scotland. However, it will be able to take action in the future should the position deteriorate".

In England and Wales, the ban has had only four and a half years to operate and is watered down by the availability of exemptions. Where it is thought appropriate, there is nothing to prevent clubs from applying to their local justices for an exemption. There may regrettably be places where the local circumstances, known to the justices, warrant refusal of an exemption. At many others, it will be granted as indeed it has been already at a number of grounds.

258. When such exemptions exist, there is no clear evidence to suggest that late arrivals are greatly reduced. Indeed, the argument that no-one can get drunk in the ground because of the problems of getting served or because only low alcohol beer is available, seems to me contradictory to the main argument. Those who wish to drink full strength beer in quantity will not be much attracted by the service offered inside the ground.

259. In these circumstances I consider it would be a retrograde or at least premature step at this time to restore a blanket licence to sell alcohol at designated sports events. I do not go so far as to suggest that the total ban applicable in Scotland should be extended to England and Wales *ie* that no exemptions should be available. But I do not believe it appropriate to relax the present restrictions.

260. Are there other steps which could and should be taken to reduce problems from excessive drinking?

Arrests

261. I have referred to the provision in Section 2 of the 1985 Act making it an offence to be in, or to attempt to enter, a designated sports ground whilst drunk or in possession of intoxicating liquor. The impact of these provisions clearly depends upon enforcement. Here again there is a contrast between Scotland and England. In England, although arrests are made, there is a tendency to eject many offenders without arresting them. In Scotland the police take a firm line. They do not eject offenders; they arrest them. The English approach may partly be due to a commendable desire not to be seen as hostile to football spectators. However, it is also a matter of expediency. Making an arrest requires the arresting officer to take the offender to a police room and go through the prescribed procedure and paperwork. This takes the officer away from his post for a minimum of a quarter of an hour. At some grounds (Hillsborough was one) evidence suggests a much lengthier absence is common. Clearly, if a serial of eight officers is posted to a bank of turnstiles, three or four arrests may greatly reduce the team for a significant period. There is a tendency, therefore, to avoid making arrests save in the worst cases. I do not wish to advocate repressive measures which would be counter to all I have said about the need for a new attitude towards spectators. On the other hand, it cannot be a good ground for declining to make an arrest that one cannot spare an officer to do it. **I therefore recommend that consideration be given to streamlining arrest procedures so as to divert an arresting officer from his post for the minimum time.** One method I have seen adopted is for the officer to give only basic details of the arrest and be photographed with the offender before resuming his duties. He can then return after the match to complete the documentation.

Closing Bars

262. In some areas, bars in the vicinity of the ground are closed either throughout a match day or between certain hours. This may be required by the Justices or it may be the result of agreement between police and publicans. Such a measure may however have limited effect. To close the pubs in a radius of one or two miles of the ground simply diverts drinkers to bars outside that range and may aggravate late arrival. Moreover, beer from shops with off-licences probably accounts for as much pre-match drinking as that bought in bars. This said, it may well be sensible to limit the availability of alcohol especially before a high-risk match. How effective the measure can be depends on the locality. In London or other large cities it could have little impact; in a more isolated town it could be very effective.

Early Kick-Offs

263. Traditionally, kick-off at football matches has been at three o'clock. That may formerly have been to accommodate those who worked on Saturday mornings. By another tradition, permitted hours in pubs led to a recognised drinking period from mid-morning until three o'clock. The combination of these two traditions often brings fans to a match with too much drink on board. **There is therefore much to be said for an early kick-off especially in a high-risk match.** It gives less opportunity for prolonged drinking sessions immediately

before the game. A mid-day kick-off gives time for away supporters to reach the ground but less time for early arrivals to kick their heels and lift their elbows in bars.

264. It is true that an early kick-off will discharge the fans earlier at the end of the match. Some anxiety has been expressed as to whether drunkenness avoided before and during the match may have more hours to build up after the game causing problems for the police and the local community in the evening. This could be so, but there are two moderating factors. First, drunken behaviour in the town, although a problem for the police, is less likely to cause serious danger to many people than at a match where it may be compounded by excitement, partisanship and incidents of the game and where large numbers are in a confined space. Secondly, the segregation exercise often results in the bulk of away supporters being escorted back to their road or rail transport as soon as the match is over rather than lingering in the town.

Sunday Matches

265. **Sunday matches ought also to be a considered option**. On a Sunday, there is less traffic, especially commercial traffic, to compete with those arriving for the match. Arrival, parking and departure are therefore easier for them in private coaches and cars. It is true that public transport generally on a Sunday is less plentiful but special arrangements are often made for major events. Again, bars and indeed many places of entertainment being closed on Sundays, there is less incentive to have a night on the town after a Sunday game.

CHAPTER 7

TICKETS AND TOUTS

Information on Tickets and Signs

266. It is vital to good crowd control that those attending a sports event should have clear directions where to go. It makes for confusion and hence added problems for stewards and police if spectators are milling about looking for their appropriate entrances. The congestion at Hillsborough was aggravated by poor information on the tickets and poor signposting outside and inside the turnstiles. **I therefore repeat my recommendations that tickets and signs should provide simple, clear and consistent information to spectators.**

267. All available measures should be taken in the printing of tickets to prevent forgeries being produced.

Computer Record of Tickets

268. **It would greatly help to defeat forgery and theft of tickets as well as assisting in the apprehension of those misbehaving in the ground, if clubs maintained a record on computer of ticket sales.** This is done in Italy where season tickets and tickets for all-ticket matches in seated areas are numbered and a record is maintained of the names and addresses of purchasers. Such information is of great value to the police in identifying forgeries and tracing offenders. Clearly, season tickets for seats could be made attractive if favourable terms were offered (especially to young supporters). This would enable the authorities to know for a whole season who was occupying a particular seat. As seating accommodation increases this would give greater information and control.

Fans Without Tickets

269. One problem which creates difficulties for the police is the arrival of would-be spectators without tickets at an all-ticket match. Although I found there was not a large body of such fans at Hillsborough there undoubtedly were some. At other matches the numbers have not only been large; they have been determined to gain entrance by one means or another. If they could not acquire tickets at the ground they have created so much trouble that the police have judged it best to let them in. Sometimes this has been for payment; on occasions, even free. The rationale has been that it is better to have troublemakers inside the ground where they can be monitored than roaming round the town at large. Obviously, the practice of admitting fans without tickets has a bad knock-on effect. Bands of fans unable to get tickets believe that if they turn up and create sufficient clamour the police will admit them.

Police Policy

270. This must not be allowed to continue. It is intolerable that those with no tickets should be able to blackmail their way into a ground. "If you don't let us in we'll force the gates or wreck your town", is not a threat to which a police force should submit. The policy of admitting such people is also unfair to those who have taken the trouble and spent money to buy tickets. It further involves, at a capacity match, letting in fans for whom there may be insufficient space. It may also create problems of segregation. Above all, it is allowing the mob to rule.

271. True, I held that in the crisis which developed at the Leppings Lane turnstiles on 15 April 1989, opening gate C was justified since life would otherwise have been at risk outside the ground. However, that was a matter of life and death. It arose because of inadequate facilities and inadequate crowd control. I would hope such a situation will never recur. If anything like it should recur, preservation of life must clearly be paramount. **But when the police have an option to let fans without tickets in or keep them out, their policy must clearly be to exclude them.** Unless that rule is firmly and universally applied and known the problem will grow.

All-ticket Matches

272. All the evidence I have received suggests that great caution should be exercised before making a match all-ticket. To do so can assist in achieving segregation. In general, it should however be done only where a capacity or near capacity crowd is expected. There should then be little difficulty in selling all the tickets in advance. The point of making such a match all-ticket is to prevent the arrival of greater numbers than the ground can accommodate. However, if a less popular match is made all-ticket, it may turn out that only a modest proportion of the tickets is sold in advance. If then fans arrive without tickets, they will be aggrieved at being turned away when there is space available. Moreover, the club will be tempted to give in to them and sell tickets on the day. This discredits the all-ticket policy and may cause breaches of the segregation strategy. **I therefore recommend that all-ticket matches should be confined to those at which a capacity or near capacity crowd is expected and that, having so designated them, clubs maintain a firm policy of not selling tickets at the match.**

Touts

273. The recommendations in the last two paragraphs are designed to deter those without tickets from turning up at matches and so obviating any trouble they may be tempted to cause. However, many fans without tickets turn up at the ground in the hope of buying them from touts.

274. During my visits to sports grounds I have found universal condemnation of touts by all involved in organising and managing large stadium events. Apart from the obstruction they themselves cause, touts attract fans without tickets to attend at grounds in the hope of getting in. Moreover, they sell tickets to all comers regardless of their allegiance. Thus tickets for the home area at a soccer match fall into the hands of away supporters and vice versa. The result is to frustrate the efforts of clubs and police to achieve peaceful segregation. Pockets of alien affiliation planted amongst home supporters form a focus for hostility and often violence results. Apart from these objections, voiced by the FA, the FL, the police and the clubs, most supporters also detest touts because they often corner the market for a popular match and offer tickets at grossly excessive prices.

275. From all these quarters the plea is to take positive action against ticket touts at football matches. I am mindful of the need for caution before advocating a law limiting liberty to conduct oneself and one's business freely and according to established practice. I likewise accept that market forces should, in general, operate freely in the commercial field. Nevertheless, I am satisfied from what I have read, heard and seen that outside football grounds the presence and activities of touts have a grossly anti-social effect leading both directly and indirectly to disorder. Directly, through obstruction and the attraction of numbers without tickets. Indirectly, because of trouble from those so attracted who, in the end, cannot or do not buy tickets and from those who buy their way into an opposition enclave.

276. Touts operate, of course, at places other than football grounds. They are to be found, for example, at national rugby stadia, at the All England Lawn Tennis Club at Wimbledon and at countless other sporting events. Depending on how one defines "touting", the activity could include selling unwanted tickets for the opera, the theatre or concert halls. Touting usually means, however, not just selling at face value a ticket you cannot use, but selling numbers of tickets at an inflated price as a commercial venture. There is a clear distinction between the impact of touting at football grounds and elsewhere. Football is the only sport at which segregation is practised to prevent violence. This is because it is the sport where violence inside and outside the ground is, at present, most prevalent. There are therefore strong grounds for regarding football as a special case as the Government has recognised by promoting the Football Spectators Act.

277. Whatever the policy merits of freedom to trade and market forces, they must surely yield to the maintenance of safety and the prevention of disorder. Touts at football matches put both at risk. At other sports and in other leisure fields the tout does not endanger safety or order to the same extent. Accordingly, whatever view one takes of him, he can be left to ply his trade there. But so far as football is concerned, in my view touting should be made unlawful. The fast buck should stop here.

278. At present, police can deal with touts only by somewhat strained and stretched use of existing laws. They arrest them for obstruction even if the physical obstruction caused is minimal. Alternatively, they make an arrest on the grounds that they suspect the tout of carrying forged tickets, although the suspicion of forgery may merely be convenient conjecture. After holding the tout during the match the police release him and the now valueless but genuine tickets are returned to him. Growing wise to this, many touts now carry only two or three tickets at a time, relying on a runner to bring up more from a "banker" standing off with perhaps hundreds of tickets in his possession. If the salesman is arrested the merchandise is not all lost. Police should not have to stretch the law to deal with a public mischief. There should be a specific prohibition which police can then enforce.

279. How to formulate a prohibition against touting at football grounds will require careful consideration and drafting. **It could be made an offence to sell tickets for and on the day of a football match without authority from the home club to do so.** Another way would be to prohibit such sales within a specified radius of the ground on the day of the match. Yet another would be to prohibit sales of tickets for a football match at more than face value. This third alternative would permit any genuine purchaser of a ticket who found he could not use it to recoup his outlay by selling his ticket outside the match. Its disadvantage would be the difficulty of proving a tout had sold at more than face value; ways would also be devised to evade the prohibition. I tend to favour the first alternative which is simple and capable of easy proof. The genuine ticket holder, finding himself unable on the day to use his ticket, and not permitted to sell it outside the ground, should be permitted to return it to the club and recover his money. Clubs should be prepared to accept such tickets in the interests of fairness and of having a law which defeats touts. If touting outside the ground is banned, fans with no tickets for an all-ticket match could have no excuse for turning up outside hoping to get in.

CHAPTER 8

POLICE STRATEGIES AGAINST HOOLIGANS

Cautious Optimism

280. I turn now to ways of curbing misbehaviour and dealing with hooligans. At the outset, I must record that there are grounds for cautious optimism about misbehaviour inside football grounds although the same cannot be said of behaviour outside and en route. Evidence I have received from various police forces, from ACPO, from the football authorities and from the clubs suggests that measures taken in the last couple of years have reduced incidents of violent misbehaviour inside grounds. Also, for the first time for decades, there has been a small but steady increase in attendances at matches in each of the last three years. This has occurred despite reductions in capacity. It is attributed by police and football authorities and by supporters' organisations to greater confidence by the decent majority of spectators that violence in the ground is under control.

281. These welcome signs must be seen in perspective. Disorder in the ground has been, for the most part, controlled not eliminated. There have still been occasional outbursts of violence in recent months. All that can be said with confidence is that the police are now much better equipped and informed to deal with hooligans than they were three years ago and their operations have been more successful in controlling disorder.

CCTV

282. In particular, the installation of CCTV has greatly improved police surveillance of the crowd both inside the ground and at the turnstiles.

283. In 1985, after the Bradford Disaster, the Football Trust made funds available to install CCTV at all first and second division football grounds. Unfortunately, the systems initially installed, although the best available at the time, proved to be of inadequate quality for identification purposes. Moreover, operators initially lacked the training and expertise necessary to make effective use of the equipment.

284. A number of clubs now have better equipment and most of the remainder of the 92 clubs in the League have applied to the Football Trust for funding to enable them to do likewise. The Football Trust, not unnaturally, wish to be sure the money will be well spent. They have therefore asked that an agreed specification should be laid down as to the quality of the CCTV to be installed. ACPO hope to provide this as soon as possible.

285. In the two years ending June 1989, about 200 operators were trained in the use of CCTV at matches. A training video is also available to all police forces.

286. Already, CCTV has had a major impact on the hooligan problem inside football grounds as well as proving extremely useful to monitor safety measures. If any trouble appears on the screen or is reported from any quarter of the ground, the CCTV can zoom in on the incident. The police can then record what occurs on colour video and on hard copy prints. Individuals can be picked out by facial appearance and the colour of their clothing. The evidential effect of such a video recording has proved formidable. It has persuaded hooligans, who would previously have sought to challenge oral evidence of identification, to plead guilty. Hooligans know cameras are keeping a roving watch and their activities in the ground are inhibited by that knowledge. Police evidence suggest that as a result of CCTV surveillance and the police strategies it facilitates, the more committed hooligans now concentrate their activities outside the ground, attacking opposing fans on their way to or from matches.

National Football Intelligence Unit

287. ACPO have for some years encouraged the development of an intelligence network nationwide. A national index of football liaison officers was set up to collect, record and pass on information about the behaviour, past and anticipated, of club supporters, especially the hooligan element. Thus, before a match, the police responsible for it can receive information from the football liaison officer in the visiting club's area as to the propensities of the visiting supporters and any known plans any element among them may have. Although this scheme has proved useful, the need was recognised for a central unit equipped with a computer to gather, record and disseminate intelligence. ACPO, in their written submission, say:–

"Hooligan gangs operate across a wide area and may of course be involved in criminal escapades in any town between their point of departure and the venue of the fixture. Furthermore, in recent times there is good evidence that they will often plan criminal violence which has nothing whatever to do with football. There is a need to overview such events to identify patterns and recognise what is behind seemingly unconnected events."

288. The National Football Intelligence Unit has now been set up. It is based in London; staff are in post; the Unit is being funded by the Home Office. It is hoped the computer will be installed shortly. The Unit will then be of great value in dealing not only with domestic football-related crime but also with hooligans travelling to matches abroad.

CHAPTER 9

OFFENCES IN THE GROUND

289. Although incidents of physical violence inside grounds are now much fewer, there remains an undercurrent of unruly behaviour which can and occasionally does result in disorder. Three activities in particular have this potential: (i) throwing coins and other missiles (ii) chanting obscene or racialist abuse (iii) going onto the pitch without reasonable excuse.

    i.   There can be no possible excuse for hurling missiles at a sports ground. It is not only dangerous in itself. It may and often does incite others to do likewise; that may and often does provoke retaliation. Violence may then escalate.

    ii.   No-one could expect that verbal exchanges on the terraces would be as polite as those at a vicarage tea party. But shouting or chanting gross obscenities or racialist abuse ought not to be permitted. If one starts, others join in, and to the majority of reasonable supporters, as well as to those abused, the sound of such chants from numbers in unison is offensive and provocative.

    iii.   Running on the pitch often provokes and is the prelude to disorder. This is not just because it interrupts the game or because it invades the hallowed turf. It is often done with the intention of attacking someone. Even if the invasion is not with intent to attack the referee, a player or opposing fans, it tempts others to follow suit. If rival fans come onto the pitch violence will probably break out. Even if they do not, there may well be violent exchanges with police seeking to repel the invaders. A fan may run onto the pitch merely to congratulate a goal scorer. But his action could well provoke opposing fans (displeased by the goal anyway) to invade the pitch with less benign intent.

290. Ought not these activities therefore to be made criminal offences? This has been raised before. Mr Justice Popplewell considered the same three activities. After discussing whether they should be made separate offences, he concluded, on analogy with the Scottish "breach of the peace", that a simple offence of disorderly conduct at a sports ground would sweep up not only the three activities mentioned above but other disorderly activities too. He concluded, at paragraph 4.74 of his Final Report, as follows:

"4.74 Quite clearly a new offence in England and Wales of disorderly conduct or breach of the peace on the lines of the Scottish common law offence, would be of substantial assistance in dealing with hooliganism. It would avoid the problem of trying to define all the different types of behaviour which give rise to disorder at football matches and would undoubtedly enable the police to take action much earlier than they can under the present law. This offence should be confined to sports grounds where the disorderly conduct is likely to have such a devastating effect on crowd safety. Disorderly conduct would clearly include throwing a missile, running onto the pitch, seeking to climb over or to pull down a perimeter fence, shining a mirror towards a batsman, throwing bottles or cans onto the field of play, or interfering with a greyhound or horse race. I suggest that it should be triable summarily and there should be a power of arrest. *I recommend, therefore, that consideration should be given to creating an offence of disorderly conduct at a sports ground.*"

291. This recommendation was not taken up. At the time Mr Justice Popplewell reported, the Public Order Act 1986 was in preparation. It created new offences relating to public order but none specifically related to conduct inside sports grounds. Evidence from the Home Office gives two reasons for this. First, it was thought wrong in principle to treat football or sports grounds as a special case. Secondly, it was apparently thought that the provisions of the 1986 Act, especially section 5, sufficiently covered the field.

292. As to the first reason, one must surely look at the nature of the mischief. The three specified activities would, of course, be an anti-social nuisance anywhere. But at a designated sports ground they are fraught with potential disorderly consequences. There is good reason therefore to treat as a special case the prohibition of these activities at such grounds. By analogy, having alcohol in one's blood over a fixed limit has been made an offence only in relation to driving, because it is dangerous to the public in that special context.

293. The second reason requires an examination of sections 4(1) and 5(1) of the 1986 Act. So far as is relevant, these provide as follows:-

"4(1) A person is guilty of an offence if he –

    (a) uses towards another person threatening, abusive or insulting words or behaviour . . .

with intent to cause that person to believe that immediate unlawful violence will be used against him or another by any person, or to provoke the immediate use of unlawful violence by that person or another, or whereby that person is likely to believe that such violence will be used or it is likely that such violence will be provoked . . .

5(1) A person is guilty of an offence if he –

(a) uses threatening, abusive or insulting words or behaviour, or disorderly behaviour . . .
within the hearing or sight of a person likely to be caused harassment, alarm or distress thereby".

294. Throwing missiles could only be caught under section 5 as "disorderly behaviour" if the additional element were proved that it was "within the hearing or sight of a person likely to be caused harassment, alarm or distress thereby". To adduce evidence of this last element may be very difficult indeed. It should surely be sufficient to show that the accused threw a missile at a football match.

295. As to obscene or racialist chanting similar difficulties arise. Although the chanting may be proved abusive or insulting it would also have to be shown, under section 4, that it was used "towards another person . . . with intent to cause that person to believe that immediate unlawful violence will be used against him etc". Proof of those elements may not be possible.

296. Under section 5, whilst again the chanting may be proved to have contained "abusive or insulting words", it may be difficult to show that this was done "within the hearing or sight of a person likely to be caused harassment, alarm or distress thereby". The words may cause nothing other than disgust.

297. Nor does section 18 of the Act help. Under the heading "Acts intended or likely to stir up racial hatred", the section provides as follows so far as is relevant:–

"18(1) A person who uses threatening, abusive or insulting words or behaviour . . . is guilty of an offence if –

(a) he intends thereby to stir up racial hatred, or

(b) having regard to all the circumstances racial hatred is likely to be stirred up thereby".

298. Racialist abuse of the kind chanted at football matches is probably not intended to stir up racial hatred. Nor could it readily be proved that racial hatred was likely to be stirred up. The effect of such chanting is to give cheap and ignoble amusement to those participating whilst causing offence and embarrassment to those abused and to the decent majority of fans.

299. For these reasons, I do not consider that the activities which Mr Justice Popplewell concluded should be the subject of a criminal offence are covered by the 1986 Act. He set out the arguments for and against legislation to prohibit them at paragraphs 4.42 to 4.74 of his Final Report. I do not rehearse those arguments. I agree with his conclusion that on balance, despite the difficulties of drafting and enforcement, these activities should be prohibited. Mr Justice Popplewell concluded that a "catch-all" offence of disorderly conduct at a sports ground should be considered. I appreciate the force of his reasoning. **However, I would prefer to see separate offences in respect of each of the three activities I have mentioned.** The object of the legislation must be not merely to prosecute offences when they occur but to deter them. If there is a specific offence of throwing missiles at a designated sports ground, a separate specific offence of chanting obscene or racialist abuse there and a third specific offence of going on the pitch without reasonable excuse there and, if full publicity is given to the legislation, hooligans will know precisely what is prohibited and that they do those things at their peril.

300. As to going on the pitch, I have a reason for recommending prohibition additional to those which convinced Mr Justice Popplewell. I have recommended lowering the level of fences and removing spikes and overhanging sections. That relaxation is made in the interests of the decent majority of supporters who have no yen to invade the pitch. To back up the lesser deterrent effect of lower fences I think it prudent to have a criminal sanction against pitch invasion.

301. I appreciate that at some sports grounds there is a tradition of running onto the pitch when the game is over simply from joie de vivre or to pat players on the back. At Murrayfield, for example, schoolboys sit on forms on the pitch side of the perimeter fencing and run on harmlessly at the end of the game. Again, going onto the pitch to escape some hazard on the terraces in an emergency should, of course, be legitimate. Accordingly, the offence should be aimed at prohibiting invasion of the pitch without good reason or reasonable excuse. The police will in this as in many other situations have to exercise sensible discretion and judgment.

CHAPTER 10

CLUB STRATEGIES AGAINST HOOLIGANS

302. Various club schemes to exclude hooligans have been undertaken or suggested.

Luton

303. In March 1985, Millwall visited Luton with a large contingent of "supporters". Widespread disorder broke out causing injuries to both fans and police. Serious damage was also done in and outside the ground as well as to trains returning to London.

304. Following this episode, Luton FC decided to adopt a Home Only Supporters Scheme excluding away supporters and allowing only Luton members and their guests to attend matches. I am grateful to the management of Luton FC and to the Bedfordshire police who explained to me the history, operation and merits of this scheme.

305. Applicants for membership normally reside within 25 miles of Luton. Those further away must justify why they wish to join. A membership card entitles the member to buy a ticket for entry, either in advance or on the day, and to bring in with him up to three guests. The card has a bar-coding and must be presented to obtain a ticket in advance. To buy a ticket on the day, the card is "swiped" through a computerised reader by the member at an outer set of turnstiles at the Kenilworth Road end of the ground. Payment for a ticket is then made at another inner set of turnstiles. Those members who misbehave are deprived of membership. A banned list is maintained on the computer. It consisted, at the time I received evidence, of only six names. If entry is attempted by using a banned card, a red light shows and the turnstile will not open. A steward then escorts the holder to an office outside the turnstiles where the problem is investigated.

306. The scheme started in August 1986. The equipment installed initially proved unsatisfactory. Some of the problems were: failure through condensation, delay whilst the reader checked the card's validity, and the fact that a Barclaycard could do the trick. After a number of attempts at rectification, this equipment was abandoned and a different firm of suppliers was engaged. I should mention that equipment from the first source was installed at Plymouth where it also failed after a number of attempts and the experiment was not pursued further.

307. The second system at Luton has proved effective after some teething troubles. It has been working satisfactorily now for nearly two seasons.

Benefits of the Scheme

308. Both the club and the police are happy with the effects of the scheme. The exclusion of away supporters naturally excludes the hooligan element which they would have included. But it also removes the focus for the aggression of any home hooligans. With no visitors to attack or bait, it is said that the hooligan elements in Luton have faded away. They have not sought to join the scheme, nor do they seem to travel to away games. The town has also benefitted. Shops which previously had to board up their windows now enjoy a peaceful Saturday trade which has increased by 40%. Arrests at matches have dropped from over 100 per season before the scheme to nil. Police costs have been greatly reduced. The club accepts that initially there was a fall in attendances, but claims they are rising again. In 1985/6, average attendance was 11,100, in 1986/7 it was 10,300, in 1987/8 it was 8,038 and in 1988/9 it was 10,039.

309. The list of benefits is impressive and there can be no doubt that the scheme has been a success for Luton. But would it be successful elsewhere?

310. Luton is, in the football context, somewhat isolated geographically from other clubs, their fans and their catchment areas. In this, its situation differs greatly from, for example, London clubs or those on Merseyside, Greater Manchester or the Midlands. Hence the assumption that those within 25 miles of Luton are likely to be natural Luton supporters. Luton also differs from clubs in the larger conurbations by size of crowds, their average numbers being only about one-quarter of those at large clubs. The banned list is tiny. An important feature of the Luton scheme is the use of outer and inner turnstiles for which the ground has ample room. Many other grounds do not.

311. At Luton, the card-holder himself "swipes" his card through. The club and the police acknowledge that, if the card had to be passed to a turnstile operator to "swipe" it through, entry would be considerably retarded. They also accept that the essential feature of Luton's success has been the ban on away supporters rather than the membership card scheme itself.

Ban All Away Supporters?

312. If this is the touchstone of success in eliminating hooliganism, why not introduce it generally and have no away supporters at any football matches nationwide? This has been considered before and rejected. Mr Justice Popplewell in his Interim Report recommended that:

"Urgent consideration should be given to introducing a membership system in England and Wales so as to exclude visiting fans".

However, in his Final Report he modified this and recommended that:

"Consideration should continue to be given to some form of membership scheme for Football League clubs in England and Wales".

313. Clearly the Government has rejected the idea of a ban on all away supporters which forms no part of the scheme of the Football Spectators Act 1989.

314. To exclude all away support would be a draconian step. It would halve the number of matches fans could attend. It would seriously diminish clubs' revenue and deprive football grounds of a healthy atmosphere of rivalry, which some say is a casualty of the Luton scheme. But perhaps the conclusive point is that it would be impractical and possibly counter-productive in the campaign against hooliganism.

315. To exclude away supporters from Luton is one thing. Those excluded can at least go at present to any other match instead. But to exclude all away supporters from all matches and especially to exclude them from "local derby" matches or matches in large cities could cause serious disorder. If Manchester City supporters could not go to Old Trafford when their team plays there, or Chelsea supporters follow their team to Highbury or to their neighbours Queen's Park Rangers, trouble could result. There would be attempts and devices to defeat the scheme and get into the ground in defiance of it. There could well be disorder outside grounds. The more fanatical supporters and the hooligans would be unlikely to stay home and play patience.

Away Members Only

316. There is a halfway house between freedom for all comers and a ban on all away supporters. This is to make entry to sections of the ground for away supporters by ticket only; tickets to be allocated strictly to members of the away team's travel club and no tickets to be available on the day of the match. This scheme builds on an existing practice adopted at some grounds for key matches, for example the Liverpool v Arsenal match in May 1989 to decide the championship. It also builds upon existing club membership schemes. Most clubs have a club membership scheme of some sort following an agreement between the football authorities and the Government in February 1987, whereby all clubs were to introduce schemes covering at least 50% of each ground's capacity by the beginning of the 1987/8 season. Compliance was patchy and varied from a membership of over 40,000 at Manchester United to one or two clubs which did nothing at all.

317. The away members only solution encourages the promotion of membership schemes offering discounts, favourable travel facilities and other benefits. It aims to limit away supporters to those, in effect, vouched for by the away club. Misbehaviour would result in loss of membership and thus exclusion from future away matches as well as loss of other membership privileges. The scheme has the unanimous approval of the 48 third and fourth division clubs, given at their annual general meeting in June 1989.

318. As with any proposed solution to the hooligan problem, this scheme cannot be watertight. It has to be recognised that any membership scheme is vulnerable to abuse arising from the loss or theft of cards and from the determined activities of those who, for whatever reason, do not possess them. The away members only scheme does at least hold out good prospects of improving behaviour in the away supporters' enclosure since only those vetted by the away club will be allocated tickets there. That may deter others from travelling but there may still be some who are determined to travel and get in. On occasion, the FA has ordered that a club's supporters having a bad record for causing disorder can be admitted at away matches only if they are accredited members of their own club. Leeds United is an example. This has, on the whole, proved beneficial. However, on occasions, Leeds non-member supporters – perhaps those living near the ground Leeds United

are due to visit – manage to get tickets intended for home supporters at or from the ground. They then get into the wrong end and cause trouble. This seems to be what happened at Ayresome Park on 9 December 1989. Much therefore depends upon the care and scrutiny given to ticket allocation by the home club. Often it is too easy for segregation plans to be thwarted by ready availability to all of tickets from the home club whether at the box office or even by credit card over the telephone. I appreciate the difficulty of identifying surely home and away supporters but clubs should review their procedures with a view to tightening them.

319. Despite its imperfections, I consider the away members only solution has some merit both in excluding undesirables from away supporters' enclosures and in encouraging the growth of club membership schemes conferring real benefits on members. It should be given further consideration.

CHAPTER 11

OTHER POSSIBLE MEASURES AGAINST HOOLIGANS

Exclusion Orders

320. At present, pursuant to Part IV of the Public Order Act 1986, a court, on convicting a person of an offence connected with football has power, in addition to imposing a sentence, making a probation order or discharging him, to make an exclusion order prohibiting him from entering premises to attend any football match. The exclusion order must be for not less than three months. If a breach is proved, the offender is liable to imprisonment for one month, to a fine or to both.

321. This provision has not made much impact. It has not been greatly used by the courts. When orders have been made they have tended to be for too short a period. On one occasion, absurdly, Justices imposed a three month exclusion order on an offender appearing before them in May! A great weakness of a bare exclusion order is the difficulty of discovering whether it is being obeyed or flouted.

322. By section 27(5) of the Football Spectators Act 1989, the provisions of the Public Order Act 1986 relating to exclusion orders shall cease to have effect when the Secretary of State, by Statutory Instrument, brings the 1989 Act into effect. So exclusion orders will go, to be replaced by expulsion from the national membership scheme under Part I of the 1989 Act and restriction orders under Part II, as I shall explain in the next Chapter.

Enforcing Exclusion by Attendance Centre Order

323. Were exclusion orders to be retained and used more realistically there are two additional measures which could be taken to enforce them. First, there could be provision for attaching to an exclusion order a requirement to attend at an appointed centre on the occasions of designated football matches. Failure to attend would immediately be detected and would render the absentee liable to further penalties including imprisonment.

324. Such a measure would have a number of merits. A mere ban on entering grounds may be flouted without detection and in any event does not ban presence near the ground. An attendance centre order would provide a means not merely to ban a hooligan from entry to a ground but to keep him physically from going there. He would thus be prevented from causing trouble outside or near the ground as well as inside it. This would be achieved without adding to the prison population, unless he defaulted, and without any elaborate scheme impinging on spectators generally. The provision would be the logical counterpart in the domestic scene to the provisions of Part II of the 1989 Act relating to foreign matches.

Is it Practicable?

325. I appreciate that detaining convicted hooligans during designated matches in the domestic football programme is a bigger undertaking and would impose a more restrictive penalty than requiring them merely to report on the occasions of English matches abroad. It is necessary, therefore, to consider the present structure of attendance centres, what extension of it might be necessary, the resource implications and the fairness of such a measure.

Attendance Centres

326. At present section 17 of the Criminal Justice Act 1982 empowers courts to make attendance centre orders for young people under 21 who:

(a) have been convicted of an imprisonable offence;

(b) have defaulted on payment of their fines etc; or

(c) have failed to comply with the requirements of a probation or supervision order.

Attendance centre orders may not be used for those who have previously been given a custodial sentence except in special (undefined) circumstances. The minimum length of an order is 12 hours, except for those under 14. The maximum is 24 hours under 17, and 36 hours for those aged 17 to 20.

327. At present there are 137 centres: 111 junior centres for those aged under 17, and 26 senior centres for those aged 17 to 20 (males only). The senior centres are, for the most part, in the larger conurbations. The Home Office has recently reviewed the use of the junior centres and some with low attendance figures are being closed.

328. Most centres are in school premises. They are normally open for 2 (junior) or 3 (senior) hours every other Saturday, usually, but not invariably, in the afternoon. Each centre is staffed by an officer in charge, normally an off-duty or retired police officer, assisted by other instructors. Regimes include physical education and at least one other activity.

329. Subject to these factors, attendance centre orders can be made at present against those convicted of football related offences. They cannot however be imposed on anyone over 21, or anyone who has had a custodial sentence.

330. Effectively to exclude the offender from football grounds, it would be necessary to have the centre open at least on every Saturday afternoon during the season. To try to include week-day evening matches would create difficulties in making centres available and might be thought too oppressive on the offender. If power to make orders were extended to cover those over 21 and those who have served a custodial sentence, the centre would have to provide for a more challenging type of offender. It would probably be thought inappropriate to mix 17 to 20 year old attenders with more hardened hooligans.

Resource Implications

331. Such an extension would probably involve an increase in the number and calibre of staff. Presently, as indicated earlier, staff include retired and off-duty police officers. More such personnel would be required. However, such increases might be modest in comparison with the police resources likely to be required to implement the national membership scheme (see paragraphs 420 to 423 infra).

Fairness

332. I would not suggest that the imposition of an attendance order should be a mandatory accompaniment to an exclusion order. It would be a discretionary power available to the courts to be used in accordance with the same criteria as apply in Part II of the 1989 Act, *ie* no such order could be made unless the court was satisfied that making it in relation to the accused would help to prevent violence or disorder at or in connection with designated football matches (*cf* section 15(2) of the 1989 Act). This would enable the courts to keep the numbers of orders within manageable limits and to apply them only in serious cases where the offender might otherwise be in danger of a custodial sentence.

333. In such situations, if the offender were judged by the court to be a committed football hooligan, and were required to attend for say two hours each Saturday in the football season, to a maximum of 36 hours (ie nearly half a season) or even 72 hours, he could not surely have any just grievance. The order would be less harsh than even the shortest prison sentence and, from the public's point of view, much more effective.

334. I recognise the practical difficulties in implementing extended attendance centre orders but, if those difficulties can be overcome, the scheme would have considerable merits. I accordingly recommend that consideration be given to implementing it.

Tagging

335. A second possible measure to enforce exclusion from the ground and its environs is electronic monitoring or tagging. This device is used successfully in the United States. Pilot schemes are presently being run here by the Home Office. Accused persons on remand are kept under supervision using anklets with small radio transmitters linked to a central computer. Despite reports of some difficulty with the pilot schemes, Mr John Patten in an answer to a Parliamentary Question on 10 January 1989 stated:–

"It is already clear that the technology can be put to practical use and that the procedures for fitting the equipment and monitoring defendants are practicable. It would now be desirable to test the use of electronic monitoring on a trial basis in an area in which substantial numbers are likely to be eligible for its application as a condition of bail."

Moreover, you are reported as having said to the Bow Group on 11 December 1989:–

"There is a need for courts to have powers to make curfew orders, confining offenders to their homes at certain times. This should not be a 24 hour house arrest. They need to be able to go to work if they have a job, attend training courses or probation centres, or receive treatment for alcohol or drug misuse. But some types of crime - pub brawls, for example, or car thefts - could be reduced by curfew orders. I very much hope that our experiments with electronic monitoring will enable it to be extended from defendants on remand to sentenced offenders, so as to make a curfew order properly enforceable".

336. If the experiments do enable the tagging to be extended to sentenced offenders, it would be a most useful and effective way of ordering convicted hooligans, excluded from grounds, to remain at home during designated matches. Their obedience to the orders could be monitored without excessive resource requirements.

337. **I therefore recommend that consideration be given to using this technology in the sentencing of offenders convicted of football-related offences.**

PART IV – THE FOOTBALL SPECTATORS ACT 1989

CHAPTER 12

OBJECT AND PROVISIONS OF THE ACT

338. The principal object of the Football Spectators Act is to break the link between football and hooliganism. It aims to do this by a national membership scheme requiring spectators to purchase and hold membership cards without which they will not gain admission. Those who commit relevant offences or otherwise misbehave in a football context will be deprived of membership and thus be excluded from attending matches. It is hoped that by this strategy hooligan activity will be eliminated both inside and outside football grounds. Thus, Mr Ridley, then Secretary of State for the Environment, said at the launch of the Bill on 17 January 1989:–

"For the first time, there will be an effective and comprehensive procedure to keep hooligans away from football matches. Of course there will be attempts to abuse the system but if the scheme is effective, those attempts will fail. We believe that it offers the real prospect of ending football hooliganism both inside and outside grounds. If hooligans know that they will not be allowed into football matches, they will have no incentive to travel to them. The link between football and hooliganism will be broken and football will cease to be a focus for violence."

Provisions of Part I

339. The Statute is an enabling Act and permits the Secretary of State to make an order by Statutory Instrument to bring it into operation (section 27(2)). I do not propose to set out all the provisions of the Act in every detail. In the broadest terms, however, Part I of the Act is to the following effect.

340. Section 1(5) provides for a national membership scheme ("the scheme") to restrict "the generality of spectators attending designated football matches to persons who are members of the scheme". Section 1(2) gives the Secretary of State power to designate football matches or an individual match.

341. Two new bodies are to be appointed by the Secretary of State. The first is the Football Membership Authority (FMA), a corporate body with articles of association. The FMA is to be responsible initially for drafting the scheme (section 4(1)). The Secretary of State is empowered to approve the scheme, again by Statutory Instrument (section 4(3)). The FMA is then to be responsible for the administration of the scheme (section 3(1)). Section 7 disqualifies from becoming or continuing to be a member of the scheme anyone subject to an exclusion order under section 30 of the Public Order Act 1986 (after conviction of an offence connected with football) whilst he is so subject. Also, anyone convicted of a relevant offence, being one of those listed in Schedule 1 to the new Act, is likewise disqualified. Anyone so convicted is disqualified for five years if he receives an immediate prison sentence and for two years if not.

342. The second body is a quango to be called the Football Licensing Authority (FLA) (section 8). The FLA is to be responsible for the grant (section 10(1)) or refusal (section 10(3)) of a licence to admit spectators to any premises to watch any designated football match there. It has power to impose conditions on the licence (section 10(4) to (7)), to make inspections and inquiries (section 10(8)) and to vary a licence (section 10(10)), suspend or revoke it (section 12). In making decisions under section 10, the FLA is to have regard to whether the equipment, the premises and the responsible persons there are such as to secure compliance with the scheme.

343. The FLA also has ancillary functions, as noted earlier; first, to include in a licence, if the Secretary of State so directs, a condition as to seating (section 11); secondly, to keep under review and oversee the discharge by local authorities of their 1975 Act functions regarding football grounds and Safety Certificates (section 13).

Contents of the Scheme

344. Section 5(2) prescribes as follows:–

"The scheme must include provision –

(a) securing that the only spectators permitted to attend at designated football matches are authorised spectators;

(b) providing for temporary membership of the scheme, including (in particular) the temporary membership of football club guests;

(c) providing for the admission as spectators at designated football matches, without their being members of the scheme, of –

(i) disabled persons, and

(ii) accompanied children,

in such circumstances and subject to such conditions as are specified in the scheme;

(d) securing that persons who are disqualified under section 7 below are excluded from membership while so disqualified;

(e) providing for the exclusion from membership, for an appropriate period not exceeding two years determined under the scheme, of persons who are, by reference to circumstances specified in the scheme, determined under the scheme to be unfit for membership and for notifying persons who are excluded from membership of the grounds for the exclusion;

(f) imposing pecuniary penalties on any persons having functions under the scheme for failure to discharge those functions;

(g) imposing requirements as respects the procedure to be followed in dealing with applications for membership of the scheme and requiring that in Wales any application form for membership of the scheme shall also be available in Welsh;

(h) imposing requirements on responsible persons as respects the procedure to be followed and equipment to be used in relation to any designated football match to secure that, except in an emergency, the only spectators admitted to and permitted to remain on the premises are authorised spectators;

(i) to such effect, in relation to the admission of spectators to the premises, as the Secretary of State may specify in writing;

(j) establishing and maintaining a central register of members of the scheme;

(k) regulating the form and contents of membership cards; and

(l) establishing procedures for the making and consideration of representations against decisions made under the scheme refusing or withdrawing membership of it and for the independent review of the decisions in the light of the representations;

and in this subsection "accompanied children" means persons under the age of 10 years in the charge of an authorised spectator."

345. Section 5(3) prescribes, inter alia, that the scheme may make provision for the imposition of charges for membership cards (section 5(3)(b) and by section 5(3)(c)):-

"for the admission as spectators at designated football matches, without their being members of the scheme, of descriptions of person specified in the scheme in such circumstances and subject to such conditions as are so specified".

346. My short summary of Part I omits a number of provisions eg the constitution of the FMA and of the FLA, details of offences, defences to them and appeals, Data Protection Act 1984 implications etc.

Provisions of Part II
347. Before proceeding to discuss the implications of Part I of the Act, which are highly controversial, I should refer to the provisions of Part II which are not. Although I assume my remit is limited to sports events within the jurisdiction to which Part I applies, the scheme of Part II is, I think, relevant.

59

348. The aim of Part II is to prevent convicted hooligans from travelling to matches abroad including matches in Scotland and there by misbehaviour causing trouble and damaging our national reputation.

349. The scheme, again stated in broad terms, is to give courts power to make a restriction order after a conviction for a relevant offence, in addition to any other sentence (section 15). Such an order is to be for five years if it accompanies an immediate sentence of imprisonment; otherwise for two years (section 16(1)). It imposes a duty to report at a police station (unless exempted) on the occasion of designated football matches abroad. Failure so to report is an offence punishable on summary conviction by up to one month's imprisonment, by a fine or by both (section 16(5)). There is provision in section 22 for making restriction orders consequent upon convictions in countries other than England and Wales for "corresponding offences" to those listed in Schedule 1.

350. Even those implacably hostile to the provisions of Part I are mostly in favour of Part II. In my view it is a sensible and practicable measure to take against a persistent mischief practised by a small minority but with national repercussions. To adapt a famous dictum, never in the field of sport has so much odium been brought upon so many by so few. The scheme is aimed directly and solely at the few whose misbehaviour abroad brings such odium upon English football supporters generally. I welcome it.

CHAPTER 13

THE NATIONAL MEMBERSHIP SCHEME

351. Returning to Part I, it is crucial to a full evaluation of its likely impact to know the terms of the scheme to be approved. At present there is no approved scheme, nor even a draft scheme, since the FMA has not yet been appointed, although the FA and FL have been offered "first refusal" for appointment as such. I do not know therefore how and in what terms such a scheme would comply with the requirements of section 5 set out above.

352. The only guide presently available is the Invitation To Tender (ITT) and the Statement Of Requirements (SOR) prepared by Ernst & Young, Management Consultants, in conjunction with the Department of the Environment. This document is directed to companies which have shown interest in tendering for the contract to supply the relevant technology. The ITT was dated 1 December 1989 and required tenderers to respond by 19 January 1990. As I write this report that date is still ahead and so the response is not known. Presently there are seven potential tenderers.

General Requirements of the ITT and SOR

353. The successful tenderer will be required to set up, manage and operate a company, the "scheme operating company" (SOC) to run the entire scheme. It will work under the overall policy, supervision and control of the FMA. At the outset of the ITT, certain key objectives have been identified as follows:-

" 1. Minimise the turnstile process time and the queuing problems that might occur in large crowds close to kick-off and keep them within acceptable limits.

2. Fund the scheme, taking account of its costs and also the possible disincentive effect to supporters of paying membership fees.

3. Ensure the application process, card production and issue procedures meet the requirements within acceptable turnaround times to spectators.

4. Deal with invalid card holders at entry points and ensure that offenders against the membership rules are dealt with fairly and that any punishment can be enforced.

5. Keep within manageable limits the size of the referral file containing banned members to ensure that speed of access to it is acceptable and still have sufficient protection against the use of lost, stolen, forged cards and pass-backs on match days."

354. The SOR provides as follows:–

"Apart from ensuring financial integrity and acceptability of the marketing strategy, the FMA will be concerned to ensure that:

1. the number of supporters is maximised while recovering the cost of the scheme

2. the scheme does not add to problems outside grounds

3. the scheme assists in reducing hooliganism."

That the scheme must be self-funding is further stressed in the ITT as follows:–

"The Football Membership Scheme will be self-funding, that is, the SOC will be responsible for all costs and expenses (including set-up costs) incurred in carrying out its obligations under the contract and shall reimburse the FMA for expenditure incurred by the FMA both on the SOC's behalf relating to the scheme and in respect of the FMA fulfilling the requirements of the Act.

The costs of running the FMA will also need to be recovered from the income generated by the SOC.

The levels of membership fees including any variations over the period of the contract, will be subject to the prior approval of the FMA".

Ground Modifications

355. As to the cost of ground modifications, the ITT notes:

"It is anticipated that there could be a significant cost involved in accommodating the membership validation system at some grounds. Therefore any modifications to be made to the existing turnstile equipment and the inclusion of any new turnstiles should be entered against this item."

Applications for Membership

356. Applications for membership of the scheme must be made in person, not by post, using a standard application form. The form will include personal particulars and the type of application. This may be for adult membership, renewal, replacement, change of details, temporary, junior or senior membership. The form will state the membership period (normally two seasons), the applicant's nominated club allegiance, second club allegiance and national allegiance. It will include a box to allow exclusion from any mailing lists. The Post Office and the clubs will act as collection points for handling applications and carrying out an initial verification process. This will require the applicant to produce evidence to prove identity and one or more passport standard photographs. The collecting agent will be responsible for checking the form, the acceptability of the photographs and their general likeness to the applicant as well as the other evidence of identification. He will also accept the fee.

357. The SOR provides:–

"Vetting of applications at the point of presentation in a collection agency must be consistent and methods to ensure that vetting procedures are followed must be employed. The integrity of the system as an anti-hooligan measure will depend on this vetting procedure."

358. The SOR states that the major problem in handling the application will be to ensure that the attached photographs are linked to the application details to enable the subsequent correct printing of membership cards.

Validation Procedures

359. I concentrate on applications for adult, junior or senior membership. In these cases, the SOR provides two basic validation procedures which must be followed. The first is a "person check", explained as follows:–

"The purpose of this check is to stop supporters getting more than one membership card. The reason being that a ban on one membership registration would still leave the supporter in possession of another membership card. Therefore there will be both a name and an address check against the membership registration database (postcoding of all addresses will obviously make this procedure a lot faster and it may be necessary to insist upon postcodes from the start). Also it is not sufficient to undertake a straight name and address check due to different ways to spell names and addresses. The prime contractor should propose methods to ensure that adequate checking is undertaken against deliberate multiple applications."

360. Secondly, there must be a "referral file check". The referral file will contain particulars of the following:

" – persons banned from membership (existing members)

 – persons who are considered to be undesirable due to their past record who have not yet applied for membership (this will include those with existing exclusion orders against them)

 – lost/stolen membership cards either by direct notification or due to an application for a replacement card

 – fraudulent copies."

Provision and Updating of Information to Clubs

361. The national referral list will be communicated to all 92 League clubs. Moreover, the list will have to be updated weekly during the football season to add fresh instances of any of the four categories of exclusion mentioned in the last paragraph; also, to remove from the list those no longer excluded *eg* after a successful appeal.

62

362. Each club will also be given the names of those successful applicants who have claimed allegiance to the club. From this information the club will be required to keep a register of its own members.

Exploitation of the System

363. The ITT provides for the FMA by itself or a designated agent to be responsible for approving and co-ordinating the SOC's commercial exploitation of the National Membership File and extracts from that file. This is said to be "in order to protect and promote the reputation of football to avoid any possible conflict with existing and future commercial activities at a club and national level". The FMA may also licence clubs to use data relating to members who express allegiance to that club on terms and conditions to be agreed.

Membership Cards

364. It is mandatory that the membership card must carry a photograph of the member, the member's name, full membership number, the expiry date, club allegiance if any and national allegiance. The membership number must be in a "machine readable form on the card as it is the only method of rapidly enough matching the card against the national referral file".

365. The card will need to meet standards for size and durability; it will need to last for more than the normal membership period (two years) as this may be increased later.

366. The security level must ensure that:

" – cards are not forgeable

  – photographs cannot be replaced

  – machine readable membership numbers cannot be changed

  – printed details on the cards cannot be changed

  – supplies of blank cards are held in a secure environment."

All of this assumes that the membership cards "will be the 'plastic credit-card' type".

Entry Checking Procedures

367. I now come to requirements having a critical bearing on safety and crowd control. They concern the checks and procedures at turnstiles. The following six provisions are mandatory:

  i   A spectator must present a valid current membership card to the turnstile operator.

  ii   "A spectator must be authorised to hold the membership card and be permitted to attend the designated match. (Note: it has been accepted that the turnstile operator will not be able to compare the photograph on the card with the person presenting the card as well as undertaking electronic checking)."

  iii The card must not be "present on the referral file" and

  iv   can only be used "once per designated match."

  v   "The turnstile operator must not let any person into the match without them (sic) producing a membership card and validating that card using the procedures and equipment provided."

  vi   "The system should be capable of directing members into their permitted sections of the ground, using the primary and secondary club allegiance field (unless playing each other) in the membership number to determine through which entry points the member may pass."

Turnstile Alarm

368. If a card fails any of the six basic checks summarised above, the system must alert the officials (stewards and/or police). It must also be capable of alerting the turnstile operator but not alerting the spectator while in the turnstile.

369. Three types of failure are envisaged.

(1) Referral file check shows the card is subject to a ban; card notified as lost or as stolen; alternatively, the card has been used previously at that match (pass-back).

(2) Equipment/card malfunction, membership expired, temporary card not valid for match.

(3) Card being presented at the "wrong" turnstile or no card at all.

Detection

370. The procedure to be followed in relation to each of these three types of failure is mandatory and important in the evaluation of the scheme for safety and crowd control.

371. If the failure is of type (1):–

"The suspect should be apprehended and taken to an investigation area either inside or outside the ground. These will be situated at convenient places around the ground. It is anticipated that there will need to be one investigation area on each side of the ground, although this is likely to depend on ground conditions".

If the failure is of type (2):–

"The card will be retained at the entry point and a receipt for the card given to the spectator. This receipt will contain either the membership number or some method to identify the retained card later. The spectator will be advised to contact the club after the match when the problem may have been resolved".

If the failure is of type (3):–

"The spectator is turned back from the entry point".

System Contingency

372. Systems at turnstiles must be capable of operating "a degraded service" in the event of system malfunction. This must include replacement of any malfunctioning unit within five minutes and alternative power supplies if the system relies on external power. If cabling is used it must be tamper proof and more than one route must be provided between "every turnstile installed unit" and the processing unit. Turnstile systems must not depend on a single club computer system.

Performance and Environmental Conditions

373. Finally, two mandatory provisions are laid down which are of great importance to safety and crowd control.

374. As to performance the SOR provides:–

"It is critical that the conducting of the six basic checks and any follow-up procedures described in this and the next section must give rise to no significant delays to ground entry at turnstiles. The maximum additional time which will be considered will be no more than 1 second per entry to the normal ground entry rate for a particular turnstile and ground configuration at all times".

375. As to environmental conditions, the provision is:–

"Any systems installed at turnstile locations will have to operate reliably in the conditions experienced in an outdoor, all-weather, all-year environment. Power supplies to turnstiles will be unreliable."

Summary

376. As with my analysis of the statutory provisions, this summary of the contents of the ITT and SOR is not exhaustive. It seeks only to indicate how the scheme is intended to work and what is expected of it.

CHAPTER 14

ARGUMENTS RAISED BY CRITICS OF THE SCHEME

377. Having summarised the intended objects and benefits of the scheme and the means by which it is required to achieve them, I turn now to the arguments against the scheme raised by its critics.

(i) *Disproportionate?*

First, it is said that the scheme with all its complex ramifications is out of proportion to the problem. Setting up the technology and maintaining it secure and in working order; adapting grounds to install it; dealing with millions of applications swiftly; issuing millions of cards, renewing them, coping with lost and stolen cards; setting up a referral list, distributing it and updating it; training staff; coping with banned cards and other failures at the turnstile; processing offenders; dealing fairly with appellants – these, and other ancillary measures, amount to an enormous undertaking. It is aimed principally at keeping hooligans out of the ground, but, so it is said, the problem inside grounds is less than it was and could be met by other less complex and less ambitious strategies.

(ii) *Unfair?*

In aiming to exclude a minority of hooligans from the football scene, it is complained that the huge majority of decent spectators are to be put by the scheme to trouble and expense. Each fan will have to go through the application procedures, presenting his form, proving his identity, purchasing and producing photographs. He will have to pay between £4 and £10 a year to join the scheme in addition to paying for match tickets. He will have to keep his card, remember it on match days, guard it from loss and theft, and renew it from time to time for further payments. Should he forget it, or lose it, should it be stolen or become damaged, he will be put to trouble to replace it and to gain entry to matches meanwhile. It is argued that measures against hooligans should target the hooligans only, not inconvenience millions of spectators in the hope of weeding out a few.

(iii) *Casual Spectators*

There is anxiety that the scheme will, in effect, exclude from football the spectator who attends only on a casual basis or for a rare match which takes his fancy. Such a spectator, it is argued, would not go to the expense or trouble (especially the latter) of buying a membership card simply to attend an occasional match. This category of spectator is thought possibly to account for some 20% of present attendances – sizeable numbers to be deprived of their present freedom to watch football.

(iv) *Diminished Club Revenue*

Taking these lost casual visitors together with former regular attenders who may also find the scheme a disincentive, the clubs fear their revenue will be severely reduced. For this reason, inter alia, they have been strongly opposed to the scheme.

(v) *Danger of Congestion and Disorder*

There is concern that the ambitious technology, which is yet to be produced and tested, may fail. Alternatively, that even if, by persistence and through trial and error, it could in the end be made to function reliably, there may be serious failures in the teething period. In either of these events the fear is that congestion at the turnstiles could cause serious danger or disorder.

(vi) *Will the Scheme Defeat Hooligans?*

Even if the technology works according to plan, will it (a) exclude determined hooligans from inside the ground and (b) also induce them to stay away from the environs of the ground? The criticism is that it may do neither of these things, especially not the latter.

(vii) *Police Resources*

There is concern, especially from the police themselves, as to the numbers of police to be deployed and the facilities they will need at the ground to cope with problems arising from the scheme at the turnstiles. These will involve banned cards, lost cards, stolen cards, unreadable cards and determined hooligans trying by various means to buck the system.

In short, critics say the scheme proposes a sledgehammer to crack a nut; a sledgehammer which may not swing at all but, if it does, may not swing safely or even reach the nut.

Arguments Relevant to this Inquiry

378. Of the seven arguments I have just briefly summarised, the first four do not bear directly upon safety or crowd control. They may have considerable force and (ii) and (iii) do bear upon matters considered in Part I of this Report (especially better treatment of spectators). However, they raise issues of policy which are essentially for Parliament. Accordingly, I say no more as to those four points.

379. On the other hand, arguments (v), (vi) and (vii) do bear very relevantly upon safety and crowd control. They are therefore within my remit and I shall explore them in turn.

CHAPTER 15

DANGER OF CONGESTION OR DISORDER

Present Risk of Congestion

380. Congestion outside turnstiles and consequent injuries or disorder are already recognised risks. Those risks are aggravated by the limited number of turnstiles available and the limited scope for increasing them at many old grounds. They are also increased by the late arrival of a large proportion of the crowd, which is a common occurrence.

381. During the last busy 20 minutes before kick-off, queues, or sometimes a phalanx, of waiting spectators, tend to build up. If the delivery through the turnstiles is delayed or slowed down, that build-up grows and its pressure further retards the turnstile operation. The next stage is that those waiting become restive, fearing they will not get in for the kick-off. Crowd noise from the ground, denoting that the teams are out, increases impatience. There is then real danger of pressure towards the turnstiles causing injuries and panic causing disorder. This is what happened at Hillsborough. It is said that it nearly happened again, despite Hillsborough and the interim recommendations, at Coventry on the first day of the new season.

Additional Time to Check Cards

382. These risks have existed even without a national membership scheme. Since the scheme requires that all spectators passing through the turnstiles must produce their membership cards for checking, it is inevitable that some additional time will be taken for each spectator.

383. In realistic acknowledgement of the risk this might create, the ITT states as its first key objective:-

"Minimise the turnstile process time and the queuing problems that might occur in large crowds close to kick-off and keep them within acceptable limits".

The SOR likewise requires the FMA to ensure:–

"The scheme does not add to problems outside grounds".

More specifically, I repeat the mandatory provision of the SOR as follows:–

"It is critical that the conducting of the six basic checks and any follow-up procedures ... must give rise to no significant delays to ground entry at turnstiles. The maximum additional time which will be considered will be no more than 1 second per entry to the normal ground entry rate for a particular turnstile and ground configuration at all times".

384. Even if this is achieved, it would reduce the numbers per hour admissible through a turnstile from the norm of 500 (mentioned in Appendix 3 at paragraph 33) to about 436.

385. But *can* it be achieved? This depends upon two factors: (i) what has to be done at the turnstile; (ii) whether the technology can achieve the required rate; not only in favourable conditions but in real life and despite attempts to defeat it.

(i) *Procedures at the Turnstiles*

386. The six entry checks which have to be undertaken at the turnstile (see supra paragraph 367) require the spectator to "present a valid current membership card to the turnstile operator". So, in the normal case, there will be a passing of the card to the operator, a validation of it by him, and a return of the card to the holder – all of this to be additional to buying a ticket or (at an all-ticket match) presenting a ticket and having the stub returned.

387. The system as prescribed in the ITT depends upon the operator getting possession of the card because it has to be "retained" at the turnstile if there is a failure of type (2) eg malfunction or card expired. This requirement is significant when one is dealing with a time factor not to exceed 1 second. The scheme is unlike that at Luton, for example, which must be quicker since (a) there are two sets of turnstiles with an operator only at the inner set and (b) the member swipes his own card through at the outer turnstile. If the ITT were to be changed to follow the Luton example, however, what would happen at grounds where there is

insufficient space for two sets of turnstiles and how would the operator get possession of the card so as to "retain" it if there were a malfunction?

388. If the turnstile alarm alerts the operator to a failure of type (1) – a banned, lost or stolen card or pass-back – the suspect is to be apprehended. The turnstile operator will therefore have no more to do with him; but how long it will take to have the suspect apprehended inside or outside the turnstile will depend on the police presence to which I shall turn later.

389. If the failure is of type (2), apart from retaining the card, the operator is required to give the holder a receipt for it which "will contain either the membership number or some other method to identify the retained card later". Since the operator will be unable to anticipate the card numbers of those which fail for a type (2) reason, he cannot have a receipt ready in advance. If he has to make one out, hand it to the entrant and explain the procedure for redeeming the card later, the exercise would take considerably longer than 1 second – especially if, as would be likely, there is some backchat.

390. It is true that the SOR requirement that the scheme must add no more than 1 second to the turnstile time, although said to be mandatory and critical, could be changed. However, in my view the authors of the SOR were right to choose 1 second as "the maximum additional time which will be considered". At 500 per hour, each entrant has 7.2 seconds to go through the turnstile. *Any* additional time could cause difficulty; 1 second is an addition of nearly 14% to the existing 7.2 seconds and more than 1 second would, as the SOR says, be unacceptable.

391. If the failure is of type (3) – wrong turnstile: no card – the ITT requires that "the spectator is turned back from the entry point". The evidence I heard at Sheffield from many police witnesses, and all I have seen and read since, makes it clear that where there are queues, let alone a phalanx, trying to get someone who is wedged in the narrows of a turnstile back through those waiting is at best a slow, laborious and unpopular exercise. At Hillsborough, the crush made it impossible.

(ii) *The Technology*

392. It has yet to be shown that a computerised system can be produced which is capable, even in favourable conditions, of achieving reliably the requirements of the ITT. So far as I am aware, nowhere has a computerised system been installed to cope with the massive numbers of people, in the short period of time and in the all-weather context which will be required by this scheme, quite apart from the added problems of attempted disruption. The scheme therefore invites tenderers to break new ground. The fact that it has not been done before does not, of course, show that it cannot be done. But it does require greater caution and a more extensive testing procedure than if there were a successful precedent.

393. The only comparable exercise which has been attempted was a Football Identity Card Scheme in Holland. That failed in its early stages and has been shelved. However, I should stress that the Dutch scheme was very different from that proposed under the 1989 Act. It involved only five clubs with a bad history of hooliganism and it applied only to the away matches of those clubs. Only 25,000 cards were issued. Much depended on careful control of ticket sales. The scheme was introduced at the start of the 1989/90 season. Unfortunately, the opening matches of the season featured two of the five clubs hosting two of the others. Ticket sales were not controlled effectively, the clubs were hostile to the scheme, away supporters were admitted without tickets and supporters on both sides combined to defeat the experiment.

394. In these circumstances, I do not think that the failure of the Dutch scheme can found a fair argument against the totally different scheme proposed in the 1989 Act. What it does show is the need to make any such scheme proof against wrecking tactics.

Demonstration

395. One of the seven potential tenderers gave a demonstration to a Parliamentary group using a laboratory prototype to show the technology they could deploy. That being so, a similar demonstration was arranged for me and my Assessors. We were shown a "smart-card" and how it could be programmed and used as a football membership card. Each "smart-card" contains its own mini-computer. Much information can be stored inside it. The demonstration showed the holder passing the card over a reader and the possible responses of red, amber or green light, depending on whether the card was valid, doubtful or invalid. Advertising possibilities and other packages of benefits were also explained and illustrated.

396. I was extremely impressed by what we were shown. However, this was a single card, at a single simulated turnstile, in warm, dry, indoor conditions, without a large national referral file to be searched and without anyone trying to circumvent or wreck the system.

Police Apprehensions

397. I quote from the written evidence submitted by ACPO:–

"The question, however, which most concerns police officers relates to the efficacy of the technology. The (Act) naturally does not detail how it will work or what is required of it but, it is clear that, unless it is robust and virtually trouble-free, it will be counter-productive. In the worst case it could be massively counter-productive. At the least each turnstile must have access to a national database and must be able to survey that database almost instantaneously. The machine itself must be durable against sabotage . . . and must work without persistent fault. . . .

All our experience to date has been that computer salesmen have offered much and delivered little. The police feel that they must be involved in the specification for any technology and would need to be satisfied that it works before support could be given to this scheme. The consequences of repeated failure, hostile queues, interminable delays and the rest, are unthinkable".

Computer Reliability

398. The concern expressed in that passage about computer performance is not unduly cynical. Many people have personal experience of computer failures in one field or another. The computer "going down" at an airport causing delays at check-in, computer errors in banks, problems with computerised entrances to the London Underground, and, recently, computer "viruses", are merely a few examples. These problems continue to occur from time to time even with computer systems which have been thoroughly tested, which are widely used and have long ago passed through what was thought to be the teething period. In many cases such failures cause delay or annoyance but not danger. The technology for the present scheme, however, has not yet been through the stage of teething troubles. Moreover, the scheme could cause dangerous build-ups if the technology either failed wholly or failed to work at the stipulated rate. In the London Underground, where build-ups were occurring, a manned entrance channel has had to be provided at many stations alongside those which are computerised, as a safety valve. To have to open extra non-computerised entrances at football grounds would (unlike the Underground) scupper the system. Its whole and sole point is to exclude hooligans by computer checking.

399. In fact, the Act seems to leave it open to the FMA to include in the scheme power for a person in authority to open gates and let spectators in, whether they have membership cards or not, should an emergency arise (section 2(2), section 5(2)(h), section 5(3)(c) and section 10(12)(a)). If the exercise of that power should have to be considered, all the problems which arose outside Hillsborough would arise again – deciding whether the power should be exercised or not; if so, at what moment and by whom; making a clear decision and communicating it; coping with the in-rush and the loss of control and of segregation it may cause. If the power had to be exercised, the scheme would be discredited at that place on that day and perhaps generally.

Relaxation in an Emergency

400. I said in the last paragraph that the Act "seems to include power" to relax the turnstile requirements in an emergency. But the power is only to be inferred by implication from the four sub-sections I have cited. Nowhere is the power expressly given; nor is it said who shall exercise it or how "an emergency" is to be interpreted. The admission of authorised spectators only, and only by production of their membership cards, seems to be fundamental to the scheme. Yet there is no stipulation in the Act that cards have to be produced. No doubt this could be provided for in the approved scheme. But since anyone other than an authorised spectator commits a criminal offence by entering the ground, admitting a non-authorised spectator is a serious matter and could amount to aiding and abetting a criminal offence. It is therefore surprising that the Act does not indicate who is to have power to declare an emergency so as to admit all and sundry and in what circumstances.

Tests

401. What testing is envisaged? The ITT provides for a "system testing strategy". This is divided into "laboratory" prototypes and pilot system tests. Two clubs have volunteered and been accepted to be the pilot sites for the latter form of testing. They are Derby County and Reading. It is envisaged that at least four different levels of test will be carried out at each of the two clubs. These four levels are likely to be:

i   issue membership cards to existing members;

ii   issue cards to all home or away supporters;

iii   small all-ticket match (home and away supporters);

iv   large (near capacity) all-ticket match.

402. The ITT provides:

"Each test will try to simulate as close (sic) as possible the live situation with problem cards being used at random".

403. I foresee two problems which beset this testing procedure. First, the difficulty of making the test conditions truly simulate those which will obtain when the scheme is working nationwide. For example, only two clubs are to be used for the tests "with problem cards being used at random". Unless the computers at the two clubs have to search a referral list (whether real or simulated) as long as the national referral list may turn out to be, they will not have been adequately tested for capacity and speed. The estimated volume of "banned" cards, according to the SOR, is between 5,000 and 20,000 per annum. The estimate of stolen and lost cards is between 20,000 and 80,000 per annum. It is not clear whether "per annum" refers to the numbers on the referral file in any given year or to the number of fresh bannings, losses and thefts each year. Taking the more conservative approach, however, they could jointly amount to 100,000 per annum. Accordingly, for a realistic test, the computers at the two clubs would have to be able swiftly to pick out the "problem cards" from a list of up to 100,000 - somewhat different from the Luton list of six.

404. The size of the referral list may have an important bearing on the speed at which the technology can work. I repeat that key objective number 5 in the ITT stipulates:–

"Keep within manageable limits the size of the referral file containing banned members to ensure that speed of access to it is acceptable etc".

How is the referral file to be kept "within manageable limits"? Its size will surely depend upon the number of cards banned, lost or stolen. There can be no management control of the numbers lost and stolen and the number banned will depend on the number of convictions or acts of misbehaviour meriting a ban. The only way of keeping the number banned "within manageable limits" would be not to ban all those who may deserve it, which would bring the scheme into disrepute.

405. The SOR estimates that the number of cards which are unreadable or otherwise require investigation may be up to 3% of the cards being checked. So at a capacity match with 50,000 present, the test would require 1,500 malfunctioning cards to be randomly issued. Presumably, the number of unreadable cards would tend to grow during the first two years of the scheme as the first issue of cards accumulates damage from rough treatment.

406. Again, with pilot tests at only two clubs, the hooligans' response will be unpredictable. They may try to sabotage the scheme at the pilot clubs which would really put the technology to the test. They may, however, prefer to misbehave at some other ground where no tests are in progress. When the scheme is implemented generally, they will be unable to go to any such "other ground" and may only then make their attempts to sabotage the scheme.

Human Guinea-pigs

407. The second problem is that tests can only be carried out by using real spectators. Bank computers and other computer technologies can be tested by putting through figures, data and print-outs. This system can only be tested by putting through people. So in the very testing of whether the system may cause danger, danger may be caused.

Disruption and Sabotage

408. The whole raison d'être of the scheme is the perceived need to eliminate from football a hooligan element so substantial, and so determined to make trouble, as to justify this enormous undertaking. Since the scheme seeks to defeat such determined hooligans, it must be assumed that the hooligans will seek to defeat

the scheme. They will see it as a challenge. Wrecking or circumventing it will add a new piquancy to the perverse pleasure they derive from their activities. Mr Ridley recognised this on the launch of the Bill, in the passage I have quoted, when he said:–

"Of course there will be attempts to abuse the system but if the scheme is effective, those attempts will fail".

409. Accordingly, the technology will not only have to be capable of fulfilling the requirements of the scheme without malfunction, in all weathers and at the stipulated speed. It will also have to be resistant to the ingenuity and determination of those who may seek to sabotage it or find a way round it. It will need to do these things not just most of the time, but all of the time. This is a very tall order, and for the reasons I have set out above, I have the gravest doubts if it can be met. Should it not be met in full, the safety implications would be serious indeed.

CHAPTER 16

WILL THE SCHEME WEED OUT HOOLIGANS?

410. Even assuming that the technology can be made to work reliably and is not disrupted or sabotaged, two questions still arise on whether the scheme is likely to achieve its objects. (i) Will the scheme in fact weed hooligans out of the ground and (ii) will they also be deterred from causing trouble outside the ground or at places en route?

(i) *Exclusion from the Ground*

411. The strategy depends first upon the court banning the hooligan after conviction of a relevant offence or the FMA banning him after some misbehaviour. But to impose a ban is one thing; to enforce it is another. True, the banned hooligan will not lawfully be able to enter by presenting a valid membership card of his own, once he is on the referral list. But he may still enter by other means.

412. A serious defect in the scheme is the acceptance that the entry procedure will not involve checking the photograph on the card against its presenter. Such checking is precluded by the need for speed. But the main rationale of having a photograph of the member on his card is defeated if it cannot be relied upon to exclude someone else from using the card and will be checked only should the user later be apprehended for an offence. So if a banned hooligan can get hold of a valid card he could gain entry. Not being scrupulous by nature, he may steal one, borrow one or even buy one, for it is not unlikely that a black market in cards will develop. Despite requirements in the ITT to prevent such abuses, multiple applications and forgeries may also be successfully made.

413. It is nothing to the point to say that if a banned hooligan enters the ground by using a stolen or borrowed card and is there arrested for an assault, he will have committed not one but two offences, the assault and the unlawful entry. He could be charged with the assault even without the 1989 Act, and without his commission of the assault, the unlawful entry is likely to go undetected. Nor does it seem sound to say that if he enters and is not seen to commit an offence in the ground, all is well. At the very least, the system is brought into disrepute when he brags to his mates that he has beaten it. Police evidence suggests, moreover, that the more sinister members of hooligan gangs often do not use violence themselves, but, from a vantage point in the ground, direct the activities of others.

414. I refer again to the submission from ACPO, a body with special knowledge of the hooligan problem and of how hooligans are likely to react:-

"The success of the proposals will eventually be judged at two levels.

First, there is the question as to whether this legislation will:–

(a) progressively remove hooligans from the football grounds and

(b) deter the allegiance of those who are involved in trouble and violence but do not necessarily attend matches.

Second, and in a sense more fundamentally, the question remains whether or not the simple mechanics of processing membership cards through turnstiles can actually be achieved.

The police view over a long period of time has been that these provisions are, to a great extent, marginal to the problem, if for no other reason than they cannot exclude the possibility of fraud by people who are, by definition, hell bent upon defeating the system, and because it will take a very long time before a significant number of potential hooligans are excluded by the scheme. There are some countervailing advantages:

(i) the deterrent effect may be considerable;

(ii) the club disciplinary system may well be able to take strong action on the evidence of CCTV alone;

(iii) the game will be able to exclude many of the very worst offenders.

Nonetheless, the police view is that many of the measures that we have already taken . . . are having a significant effect and are far more critical to the problem of hooliganism".

(ii) *Elimination from the Area and Routes Near the Ground*

415. I have already noted that hooliganism inside the ground has been reduced, largely by CCTV, but has been transferred outside the ground. I refer again to the submission of ACPO:

"Two aspects of control have done much to change the nature of hooliganism. The legislation which prevented the general supply of alcohol in transit and the universality of CCTV have made a major impact. Taken together the effect has been that displays of wild aggression from hordes of drunken supporters are much less frequent. The hooligan has moved out of the camera's range and in a word, there has been "displacement" away from the terraces to the darker confines of the stadium or to other venues such as public houses and to the transit system".

416. This, together with other police evidence I have received, shows that although football generally and a match in particular provide the occasion and the focal point for hooligan activity, many hooligans do not regard it as essential to be able to enter the ground. They need the converging crowds and the inter-club rivalry or enmity of a match to set the scene for their violence. They do not need the football itself. Mr Ridley, in his observations quoted above (paragraph 338) said:–

"If hooligans know that they will not be allowed into football matches, they will have no incentive to travel to them".

However, exclusion from the ground does not necessarily remove the incentive for hooligans to turn up there.

417. I fear it may be merely wishful thinking to assume that football hooligans, banned from inside grounds, will not, if they are free to do so, turn up and cause trouble outside, in public houses or in the town. It would be surprising if hooligans of Mr Justice Popplewell's group I (paragraph 48 supra) were totally to abandon their activities of attacking and baiting away supporters just because they could not themselves get into the ground.

418. It is argued by advocates of the scheme that eliminating hooligans from outside the ground, as well as inside it, has been achieved at Luton. However, the success at Luton does not in my view bear directly upon the likely outcome of the national scheme. The main factor in Luton's success has been the ban on away supporters which removes the focus for violence. There are also the other factors already noted, the geographical position of Luton, the comparatively small attendances and the fact that the Luton scheme has operated at only one club.

419. I therefore have grave doubts whether the scheme will achieve its object of eliminating hooligans from inside the ground. I have even stronger doubts as to whether it will achieve its further object of ending football hooliganism outside grounds. Indeed, I do not think it will. I fear that, in the short term at least, it may actually increase trouble outside grounds.

CHAPTER 17

POLICE RESOURCES

420. The scheme envisages that the checking procedure at turnstiles will let valid card holders through but will produce the three types of failure already described. Each of those three types of failure may involve an offence by the person presenting the card and the first type is quite likely to do so. There will therefore have to be police present to apprehend the suspect, investigate the circumstances and, it may be, make an arrest. I have already quoted the estimated failures of types (1) and (2) anticipated in the SOR. Even assuming the estimates are correct for the grounds as a whole, there will be no means of knowing how many "problem cards" will be presented at any particular bank of turnstiles. There will need to be enough police to be able to monitor each turnstile throughout the admission period. If a banned card is presented, the entrant will need to be taken by an officer to "an investigation area". The SOR anticipates there will need to be one investigation area at each side of the ground. Presumably, staff there will be equipped with the means to investigate the problem card fully. It may then be necessary for the suspect to be arrested and processed. Whilst the officer who has apprehended him is away from the turnstile through which the suspect came, further card holders should be coming through the same turnstile at a rate of about 1 per 8 seconds or faster. There will therefore need to be enough officers to cope with further problem cards. Even if the apprehending officer merely takes the suspect to an investigation room and hands him over to officers stationed there before returning to his post, the turnover rate at the turnstiles would need a substantial number of officers. Requiring stewards to do the job may be inappropriate since arrests may have to be made. Again, if the suspect realises he may be about to be arrested, he may seek to rush off and lose himself in the crowd. So dealing with presenters of "problem cards" may have to be done solely by the police. If the scheme showed, after an initial period, that the incidence of "problem cards" had settled down to a modest number, the police commitment could be reduced. But initially, considerable numbers will be needed to perform these functions in addition to those habitually undertaken.

421. Police anxiety about this commitment of resources is summarised as follows by ACPO:

"The second level at which the technology causes concern relates to procedures following a "red light" at the turnstiles. Policing at turnstiles at present is very selective and the Police Service could not countenance providing the sort of cover which would allow for a quick response to each turnstile in the event of a problem. The only powers conferred in the Bill are on the police and on the face of it every attempt to enter which activates a "red light" suggests an offence is being committed. At Manchester United for example 30,000 people will pass through the turnstiles in just over 20 minutes before kick-off. There are about 100 turnstiles and the prospects of policing this system are absolutely daunting".

422. The example of Manchester United in that passage is confirmed by the club itself in a paper on the national membership scheme entitled "A United Perspective". At page 3, the club says:

"We have yet to be shown the computer hardware that will do the work successfully. Manchester United has run a computerised box office for more than 15 years now and it is well known that what is promised by computer companies rarely, if ever, performs to anything like its supposed potential in "real" situations where they may have had no experience. Average attendances at Old Trafford are around 40,000 but on occasions this figure can go as high as 56,000. Experience shows that around 50% arrive in the last 30 minutes before kick-off and this number increases substantially for evening matches."

423. There is a risk therefore that, at big matches, police control of procedures at the turnstiles during the last 20 minutes before kick-off, in addition to their present duties, may create serious problems. Apart from the numbers of officers needed, space will have to be found for investigation rooms. It is doubtful whether one "investigation area" at each side of a ground like Old Trafford will suffice. I therefore have strong doubts about the practicality of policing the scheme effectively.

CHAPTER 18

STRATEGIES AGAINST HOOLIGANISM – CONCLUSIONS

424. I fully understand and respect the reasons which prompted the promotion and enactment of the Football Spectators Act 1989. However, it follows from my comments in the last three chapters that I have grave doubts about the feasibility of the national membership scheme and serious misgivings about its likely impact on safety. I also have grave doubts about the chances of its achieving its purposes and am very anxious about its potential impact on police commitments and control of spectators. For these reasons, I cannot support the implementation of Part I of the Act.

Suggested Strategy

425. As has been said many times, there is no single measure which will defeat football hooliganism and even a package of measures will take time to have effect.

426. That said, the strategy I would suggest is to consider relying upon a combination of all or some of the following measures:–

(i) Developing the detection and evidential potential of CCTV and the new National Football Intelligence Unit;

(ii) Prohibiting, by creating criminal offences, three specific activities in the ground:

(a) throwing a missile;

(b) chanting obscene or racialist abuse;

(c) going on the pitch without reasonable excuse;

(iii) Extending the courts' power to make attendance centre orders, in conjunction with exclusion orders, for football related offences on occasions of specified matches so as to keep hooligans away from football grounds;

(iv) Using electronic monitoring (tagging) for the same purpose.

427. These four measures are all aimed solely at the hooligans and will impinge only on them. Moreover, (iii) and (iv) are the only measures, other than imprisonment, aimed not only at banning hooligans from the ground but also at preventing them from getting into it or near it during matches. Put together with progress towards all-seating, improved accommodation, better facilities, improved arrangements for crowd control and better training of police and stewards to achieve it, I believe these measures would give the best chance of eliminating or minimising football hooliganism.

PART V – FINAL RECOMMENDATIONS

All-Seated Accommodation

1. The Secretary of State should ensure that spectators are admitted only to seated accommodation at matches played at sports grounds designated under the Safety of Sports Grounds Act 1975 in accordance with the timing set out in Recommendations 2 to 4 below.

2. Recommendation 1 should apply with effect from the start of the 1993/4 season at high-risk matches as defined under the UEFA Regulations set out in paragraph 82 above.

3. Subject to Recommendation 2 above, Recommendation 1 above should apply with effect from the start of the 1994/5 season to all matches at grounds in the first and second divisions of the Football League, the Premier Division of the Scottish Football League, and at national stadia, subject to a reasonable extension of time in the case of a club promoted to the second division of the Football League or the Premier Division of the Scottish Football League. Standing accommodation at these grounds should be reduced annually by 20% of the present standing capacity (such present standing capacity to be calculated according to Recommendation 8 below), the first 20% deduction being effective from August 1990 so as to eliminate standing by August 1994.

4. Subject to Recommendation 2 above, Recommendation 1 should apply with effect from the start of the 1999/2000 season to all matches at all other grounds designated under the Safety of Sports Grounds Act 1975. Standing accommodation at these grounds should be reduced annually by 10% of the present standing capacity (such present standing capacity to be calculated according to Recommendation 8 below), the first 10% deduction being effective from August 1990 so as to eliminate standing by August 1999.

Advisory Design Council

5. The Football Association and the Football League should establish an Advisory Design Council whose functions should be:

(a) to conduct and marshal research into the improvement and design of football stadia;

(b) to disseminate regularly such information and expertise as they acquire in this field to members of the Football League and, on request, to other football and sports clubs in England, Wales and Scotland.

National Inspectorate and Review Body

6. (a) If Part I of the Football Spectators Act 1989 is implemented, section 13 should be brought into force giving the Football Licensing Authority the functions and powers therein specified (power to review the discharge of functions by local authorities). If Part I of the Act is not implemented or is substantially delayed, other arrangements should be made for the discharge of the functions and powers in section 13 of the Act by the appointment of a body to exercise them.

(b) In either event, the body exercising those functions and powers in relation to association football should also be entrusted with similar functions and powers regarding the discharge by local authorities of their certifying and licensing functions in relation to other sports grounds and sports entertainments pursuant to the Safety of Sports Grounds Act 1975 and Parts III and IV of the Fire Safety and Safety of Places of Sport Act 1987.

Maximum Capacities for Terraces

7. Where a viewing terrace is divided into pens or areas which are self-contained, the Safety Certificate should specify the maximum number of spectators to be admitted to each such pen or area.

A pen or area is to be deemed "self-contained" notwithstanding that it has a gate or gates affording access to another pen or area and whether such gate or gates be open or shut.

8. Each figure for maximum capacity should be assessed in accordance with Chapter 16 of the Green Guide ("the Green Guide figure") subject to the following qualifications:–

(a) the maximum density permitted under paragraphs 221 and 222 of the Green Guide (when the terrace or viewing slope is in good condition) should be 47 not 54;

(b) the minimum figure specified in paragraphs 221 and 222 (when the terrace or viewing slope materially deviates from the recommended guidelines, so as to constitute a possible hazard to individuals closely packed) should be 0 not 27;

(c) in arriving at "the Green Guide figure", proper and realistic allowance must be made for all factors which should reduce the permissible density including those specified in paragraphs 220 to 224 inclusive of the Green Guide.

9. Arrangements should be made:–

(a) to limit the number of spectators entering each self-contained pen or area to the maximum capacity figure assessed in accordance with Recommendation 8 above either electronically, mechanically, by a ticketing arrangement, by counting or otherwise, and

(b) to close off further access to such pen or area when its maximum capacity is about to be reached.

10. The maximum notional rate at which spectators can pass through a turnstile should be 660 persons per hour, not 750 per hour as stated in paragraph 47 of the Green Guide. The maximum rate for any particular turnstile must take full account of all circumstances including those given as examples in paragraph 47.

Filling and Monitoring Terraces

11. There should be a written statement of intent, agreed between the club and the police, setting out their respective functions as to crowd safety and control and in particular as to the filling of each self-contained pen or other standing area and the monitoring of spectators in each such pen or area to avoid overcrowding. Any variation of the document in respect of an individual match should be agreed in writing in advance.

12. (a) At each match, there should be on the perimeter track, for each self-contained pen or other standing area (subject to (b) below), a steward (if the club is monitoring that area) or a police officer (if the police are monitoring it) whose sole duty is to check crowd conditions in that area for possible overcrowding or distress throughout the period the area is occupied by spectators. Whoever is so appointed should be in addition to any other steward or police presence. He should have ready access to a police officer who can authorise access through gates to the pitch under Recommendation 20 below.

(b) This Recommendation need not be applied to any self-contained pen or other standing area where the spectators present, or reasonably to be expected, during a particular match do not exceed one third of the area's maximum permitted capacity, or 2,000, whichever is the lower.

Gangways

13. Gangways should be kept clear, in accordance with paragraphs 97 to 99 of the Green Guide. Gangways should be painted in a conspicuous colour whether they are sunk or not. The Safety Certificate should require that no standing is allowed in gangways and that they be painted.

Fences and Gates

14. All spikes or similar constructions on perimeter or radial fences, and any sections overhanging or returning inwards towards spectators, should be removed.

15. Perimeter fencing should be no higher than 2.2 metres, measured from the top of the fence to the lowest point at which spectators may stand, and including any wall or other foundations forming part of the perimeter boundary.

16. All police officers and stewards with duties in relation to the standing areas and especially those with duties under Recommendation 12 above, should be fully briefed and trained with regard to the recognition of crowd densities, to the recognition of signs of distress and to crowd dynamics. Training should include demonstrations at the ground and photographs, designed to enable stewards and officers to recognise different crowd densities.

17. There must be provided in any perimeter fence of a pen or other self-contained area sufficient gates of a minimum width of 1.1 metres to enable that pen or area to be evacuated onto the pitch in the time prescribed for an emergency evacuation of that pen or area.

18. All gates in radial or perimeter fences of pens or other self-contained areas should be painted in a different colour from the rest of the fence and marked "Emergency Exit".

19. Where there is a perimeter fence in front of a pen or enclosure, all gates to the pitch should be kept fully open during the period when spectators are in the pen or enclosure, wherever those in command feel that this can safely be done. Whether they be fully open, partially open or closed, they should be kept unlocked throughout the period when the pen or enclosure is occupied.

20. Each gate in a perimeter fence affording access to the pitch from a pen or enclosure should be manned by a steward or by a police officer when the pen or enclosure is occupied. Whether such manning should be by a police officer or by a steward should be decided by the Police Commander. In either event, the Police Commander should appoint one or more police officers with power to authorise access through gates to the pitch immediately in the event of an emergency.

21. Suitable and sufficient cutting equipment should be provided by the club at each ground where there are perimeter fences to permit the immediate removal of enough fencing to release numbers of spectators if necessary. Agreement should be reached as to whether the equipment should be used by police, the fire brigade or stewards. Whoever is to use it should be trained to do so. Whether to use it should be a decision of a nominated senior police officer at the ground.

Crush Barriers

22. All crush barriers should be visually inspected each year for signs of corrosion. Any barrier found to be affected by a significant degree of corrosion should be repaired or replaced.

23. The layout of barriers in each pen or terraced area should be reviewed immediately (if this has not already been done following the Interim Report) to ensure that it complies with the criteria contained in Chapter 9 of the Green Guide. If it does not, the assessment of the maximum capacity figure for that pen or terraced area, in accordance with Recommendation 8 above, should reflect the fact.

Safety Certificates

24. The Secretary of State should exercise his powers under either section 6(2) or section 15(A) of the Safety of Sports Grounds Act 1975 so as to make mandatory in Safety Certificates those conditions specified in the original section 2(2) of the 1975 Act. So far as the original section 2(2)(b) is concerned "shall" should be substituted for "may".

25. In assessing these mandatory requirements in the Certificate for a particular ground, the local authority should follow the Green Guide criteria. Once that is done, the resultant figures and terms for that ground should be specified in the Safety Certificate and no variation from them should be permitted other than by formal revision.

26. Where a local authority incorporates any provision of the Green Guide into the Safety Certificate, other than one within the scope of Recommendation 25 above, it should make clear whether that provision is to be complied with absolutely or with discretionary flexibility.

27. There should be an immediate review of each Safety Certificate (if this has not already been done following the Interim Report) by the responsible local authority, which should consult the club in respect of which the Certificate is issued, the police, the fire service, the ambulance service and the building authority. Such a review should include an inspection of the stadium. Its object should be to ensure that the operative conditions of the Certificate are complied with and to add or substitute any condition shown to be necessary as a matter of urgency following the findings and Recommendations in this Report.

28. Any local authority within whose area there exists a sports ground designated under the 1975 Act for which no Safety Certificate has yet been issued should proceed forthwith to remedy the situation.

29. Every Safety Certificate should be reviewed by the local authority at least once annually and each Certificate should require to be renewed annually.

30. Each local authority should review its arrangements for issuing, monitoring, enforcing, reviewing, amending and renewing Safety Certificates (if this has not already been done following the Interim

Report). Such review should require that there exists or is provided an accountable administrative structure whereby the functions of the local authority are regularly and effectively supervised by senior officers and elected members and decisions are properly taken in accordance with the local authority's rules.

31. To assist the local authority in exercising its functions, it should set up an Advisory Group (if this has not already been done) consisting of appropriate members of its own staff, representatives of the police, of the fire and ambulance services and of the building authority. The Advisory Group should consult representatives of the club and of a recognised supporters' organisation on a regular basis. The Advisory Group's terms of reference should encompass all matters concerned with crowd safety and should require regular visits to the ground and attendance at matches. The Advisory Group should have a chairman from the local authority, and an effective procedure. Its resolutions should be recorded and it should be required to produce regular written reports for consideration by the local authority.

Duties of Each Football Club

32. Each turnstile should be inspected and its potential rate of flow measured (if this has not already been done following the Interim Report). Thereafter, regular inspections should be made to ensure that each turnstile remains capable of admitting spectators at the rate anticipated.

33. The correlation between each viewing area in the stadium and the turnstiles serving it should be such as to ensure that all the spectators intended to be admitted to that viewing area can pass through the turnstiles within one hour. If that cannot be done, the capacity of that viewing area should be reduced accordingly. Since this Recommendation includes terms and conditions within the scope of the original section 2(2)(c)(i) of the Safety of Sports Grounds Act 1975 it should be given effect in the Safety Certificate (see Recommendation 24 above).

34. Turnstiles should be closed when the permitted capacity of the area served by them is about to be reached and arrangements should be made to ensure quick and effective communication with turnstile operators for this purpose.

35. Closed circuit television should be so installed as to enable crowd densities outside the ground, within concourse areas and in pens and other standing areas, to be monitored before, throughout and at the end of a match.

36. All signposting for spectators both outside and inside the ground should be comprehensively reviewed (if this has not already been done following the Interim Report). It should, in relation to the arrangements for each match, be unambiguous, eye-catching, simple and clear and should be designed to ensure the rapid movement of spectators to their appropriate viewing areas. Any redundant signs should be removed.

37. Information on tickets should be unambiguous, simple and clear and should correlate absolutely with the information provided in respect of each match both outside and inside the ground. Retained ticket stubs should contain information necessary to guide spectators once inside the ground.

38. Information on tickets requesting spectators to be in position by a particular time should be reviewed (if this has not already been done following the Interim Report) by clubs in conjunction with the police to ensure that it corresponds with the planned arrangements for admitting spectators to the ground.

39. Clubs should consider maintaining a record on computer of ticket sales before the day of the match, for season tickets and tickets for all-ticket matches for seated areas, containing the names and addresses of those purchasing tickets.

40. All-ticket matches should be confined to those at which a capacity or near capacity crowd is expected. When a match has been designated all-ticket, clubs should not sell tickets at the match and should take steps to advise the spectators of both clubs accordingly.

41. Each club should consult with a recognised supporters' club as to the provision of pre-match entertainment aimed at attracting spectators to the ground in good time.

42. Clubs should recruit and retain sufficient competent stewards. They should be fit, active and robust, and preferably between the ages of 18 and 55. Clubs should ensure that stewards are fully trained, aware of their duties under Annex B of the Green Guide and under the statement of intent (see Recommendation 11) and able to perform them.

43. The club should provide a police control room which is:–

(a) well placed, so as to command a good view of the whole pitch and of the spectator area surrounding it;

(b) of sufficient size for the commander, his deputy and enough officers to operate the radios, telephones and CCTV screens. There should be space for others who may need from time to time to visit the room *eg* other senior officers, club management or a member of the emergency services;

(c) well equipped with CCTV, radio and telephone facilities and, where necessary, sound-proofed against excessive crowd noise.

It should be the duty of the club to provide a room and equipment to the satisfaction of the chief officer nominated under Recommendation 44 below.

Police Planning

44. The Chief Constable of each police force in whose area there is one designated sports ground or more should nominate a chief officer to liaise with the management of each football club and local authority concerned in respect of the safety and control of crowds.

45. The Operational Order for each match at a designated sports ground, and the pre-match briefing of all officers on duty there, should alert such officers to the importance of preventing any overcrowding and, if any is detected, of taking appropriate steps to remedy it.

46. The Operational Order for each match at a designated sports ground should enable the police to cope with any foreseeable pattern in the arrival of spectators at a match and in their departure. It should provide for sufficient reserves to enable rapid deployment of officers to be made at any point inside or outside the ground.

47. Police planning should provide that ticketless fans should not be allowed to enter a designated sports ground except in an emergency.

48. Arrest procedures inside and outside designated sports grounds should be reviewed so as to keep to the minimum the period during which an arresting officer is away from his post.

49. The option to postpone kick-off should be in the discretion of the officer in command at the ground. Crowd safety should be the paramount consideration in deciding whether to exercise it.

50. Consideration in consultation with the club should be given, especially for high-risk matches, to the possibility of an early kick-off or a Sunday fixture.

51. There should be available in the police control room the results of all closed circuit television monitoring outside and inside the ground and the record of any electronic or mechanical counting of numbers at turnstiles or of numbers admitted to any area of the ground. Officers in the control room should be skilled in the interpretation and use of these data.

52. Consideration should be given to the provision of a specific training course for senior officers presently acting as Police Commanders and those in line to do so. Such a course should include training in the basic strategy of policing football matches.

53. Police authorities should review the charges they make to clubs for the costs of policing inside grounds so as to ensure that realistic charges are made. The Home Office should take steps to ensure consistency of practice, subject to local discretion and the need to have regard to local circumstances.

Communications

54. There should be sufficient operators in the police control room to enable all radio transmissions to be received, evaluated and answered. The radio system should be such as to give operators in the control room priority over, and the capacity to override, others using the same channel. Additional channels should be used, where necessary, to prevent overcrowding of the airwaves.

55. There should always be a command channel reserved solely for the Police Commander to communicate with his senior officers round the ground.

56. To complement radio communications, there should be a completely separate system of land lines with telephone links between the control room and key points at the ground.

57. Within the control room, there should be a public address system to communicate with individual areas outside and inside the ground, with groups of areas or with the whole ground. Important announcements should be preceded by a loud signal to catch the attention of the crowd despite a high level of noise in the ground. This arrangement should be prominently advertised on every programme sold for every match.

58. Use should be made where possible of illuminated advertising boards to address the crowd.

Co-ordination of Emergency Services

59. The police, fire and ambulance services should maintain through senior nominated officers regular liaison concerning crowd safety at each designated sports ground.

60. Before each match at a designated sports ground the police should ensure that the fire service and ambulance service are given full details about the event, including its venue, its timing, the number of spectators expected, their likely routes of entry and exit, and any anticipated or potential difficulties concerning the control or movement of the crowd. Such details should be readily available in the control rooms of each of the emergency services.

61. Lines of communication, whether by telephone or by radio, from the police control room to the local headquarters of all emergency services should be maintained at all times so that emergency calls can be made instantly.

62. Contingency plans for the arrival at each designated sports ground of emergency vehicles from all three services should be reviewed. They should include routes of access, rendezvous points, and accessibility within the ground itself.

63. Police officers posted at the entrances to the ground should be briefed as to the contingency plans for the arrival of emergency services and should be informed when such services are called as to where and why they are required.

First Aid, Medical Facilities and Ambulances

64. There should be at each sports ground at each match at least one trained first aider per 1,000 spectators. The club should have the responsibility for securing such attendance.

65. There should be at each designated sports ground one or more first aid rooms. The number of such rooms and the equipment to be maintained within them should be specified by the local authority after taking professional medical advice and should be made a requirement of every Safety Certificate.

66. (a) At every match where the number of spectators is expected to exceed 2,000, the club should employ a medical practitioner to be present and available to deal with any medical exigency at the ground. He should be trained and competent in advanced first aid. He should be present at the ground at least an hour before kick-off and should remain until half an hour after the end of the match. His whereabouts should be known to those in the police control room and he should be immediately contactable.

(b) At any match where the number of spectators is not expected to exceed 2,000, the club should make arrangements to enable a medical practitioner to be summoned immediately to deal with any medical exigency at the ground. He should be trained and competent in advanced first aid. The arrangements made should be known to those in the police control room.

67. At least one fully equipped ambulance from or approved by the appropriate ambulance authority should be in attendance at all matches with an expected crowd of 5,000 or more.

68. The number of ambulances to be in attendance for matches where larger crowds are expected should be specified by the local authority after consultation with the ambulance service and should be made a requirement of the Safety Certificate.

69. A "major incident equipment vehicle", designed and equipped to deal with up to 50 casualties, should be deployed in addition to other ambulance attendance at a match where a crowd in excess of 25,000 is expected.

Offences and Penalties

70. Consideration should be given to creating an offence of selling tickets for and on the day of a football match without authority from the home club to do so.

71. Each of the following activities at a designated sports ground should be made a specific offence:–

    i.   throwing a missile;

    ii.   chanting obscene or racialist abuse;

    iii. going on the pitch without reasonable excuse.

72. Consideration should be given to extending the courts' powers to make attendance centre orders for football related offences on occasions of designated football matches. The provision should be capable of imposition on an offender aged 21 or over and subject to a maximum of 72 hours in the case of an offender aged 17 or over.

73. Consideration should be given to the use of electronic monitoring (tagging) in the sentencing of offenders convicted of football related offences.

Green Guide

74. As a matter of urgency, the Home Office should set up a body to revise the Green Guide in accordance with this Report, these Recommendations and the Report of the Technical Working Party (Appendix 3).

75. In any revision of the Green Guide, the values to be achieved by way of percentage recovery after the required loading tests on crush barriers should be specified. Acceptable values for various materials should be specified.

76. When the Green Guide is revised, the need to inspect crush barriers for possible corrosion should be specifically mentioned and emphasised.

APPENDICES

APPENDIX 1

ORGANISATIONS SUBMITTING EVIDENCE TO THE INQUIRY

Abbott Mead Vickers PLC
Access Committee for England
ADT Check-In Limited
Amateur Athletic Association
Associate Member Clubs of the Football League
Association of Chief Ambulance Officers
Association of Chief Police Officers of England, Wales & Northern Ireland
Association of Chief Police Officers (Scotland)
Association of County Councils
Association of District Councils
Association of London Authorities
Association of Metropolitan Authorities
Association of Scottish Police Superintendents
B J Auditorium Design
Ballast Nedam
Bath City FC
BBT Gargini
Bechtel Limited
Bedfordshire County Council (Fire & Rescue Service)
Bettersound Systems
Blackburn Rovers FC
Bradford Metropolitan Council
British Amateur Athletic Board
British Constructional Steelwork Association Limited
British Greyhound Racing Board
British Sports and Allied Industries Federation
Building Research Establishment
Professor David Canter
Central Council of Physical Recreation
Ceresco Ltd
Chelsea FC
Chief & Assistant Chief Fire Officers' Association
Christian Science Committee on Publication for South Yorkshire
Cleveland Constabulary
Convention of Scottish Local Authorities
Cremer & Warner
Department of the Environment
Derby County FC
Derbyshire County Council
DES Electrical Systems Ltd
Ernst & Young
Feedback
Fire Brigades Union
Football Association
Football Grounds Improvement Trust
Football League
Football Supporters' Association
Football Trust
Football Writers' Association
Foster & Partners Ltd
Gwent Ambulance Service
Health & Safety Executive
Hellmuth Obata & Kassabaum Inc Sports Facilities Group
Hercules Security Fabrications Ltd
Hillsborough Family Support Group
Hillsborough Steering Committee
Home Office

Institute of Building Control
Institute for Consumer Ergonomics
Institution of Structural Engineers
Intermediate Treatment Fund
Intracard
Jockey Club
John Leighton Consultancy
Keith Monks Limited
Kenrick & Company
Kent Institute of Art & Design
Kerrypak Limited
Kolara Limited
Lancashire County Council
Lancashire County Cricket Club
Larne Branch, Liverpool FC Supporters' Club
Lawn Tennis Association
Leeds United AFC
Liverpool City Council
Local Government Review
London Borough of Brent
London Borough of Hammersmith & Fulham
London Borough of Richmond upon Thames
London Boroughs Association
London District Surveyors Association
London Fire and Civil Defence Authority
Lothian Regional Council
Luton Town FC
Mabif International
Maidstone United FC
Manchester United FC
McGregor Associates
Medics at Hillsborough Working Party (University of Liverpool)
Merseyside Area Student Organisation
Merseyside Pensioners Association
Merseyside Fire & Civil Defence Authority
National Association of Fire Officers
National Council for Civil Liberties
National Federation of Football Supporters' Clubs
National Union of Public Employees
NGRC Racecourse Promoters Ltd
Norfolk County Council
Order of St John
Parliamentary All-Party Football Committee
Police Federation of England & Wales
Police Superintendents' Association of England and Wales
Pool Promoters Association
Queen's Park Rangers FC
RAC Motors Sports Association
RAN International
RDS Technology Ltd
Recreation and Leisure Trades Association
Regional Ambulance Officers' Group
Royal & Ancient Golf Club of St Andrews
Royal Association for Disability and Rehabilitation
Royal Institute of British Architects
Royal Institution of Chartered Surveyors
Royal Society for the Prevention of Accidents
Royal Town Planning Institute
Rugby Football League
Rugby Football Union
S & P Safety

Saltcoats Branch of the Labour Party
Scottish Education Department
Scottish Football Association
Scottish Football League
Scottish Police Federation
Scottish Rugby Union
Scottish Sports Council
Selhurst Park Stadium
Sheffield City Council
Sheffield Trades Union Council
Simmons PR Communications Design Ltd
Sir Norman Chester Centre for Football Research
Sound & Communications Industries Federation
South Yorkshire County Fire Service
Southend United FC
Southwark Borough Council
Spectacor Management Group International
Sports Council
Sports Council for Wales
Sports Writers and Commentators
St Andrew's Ambulance Association
St William's Foundation
Stadiasafe
Stadium Technology International Ltd
Strathclyde Police
Summit Group plc (with The General Electric Company plc)
Synchro Systems Ltd
Tavistock Institute of Human Relations
TC Team Consult AG
Thorburn Associates
Tottenham Hotspur FC
Trent Regional Health Authority
TV AM
Union of Shop, Distributive & Allied Workers
University of Oxford, Centre for Criminological Research
Welsh Office
Welsh Rugby Union
Welsh Sports Association
Wembley Stadium Ltd
West Yorkshire Fire Service
York City FC
88-Consult bv (io)

Discussions were also held with representatives of Government Departments, municipalities, police, sporting authorities, the managers of sports stadia and football clubs, architects and stadium designers in France, Holland and Italy. Additionally, the Consular Department of the Foreign and Commonwealth Office obtained information about sports stadia and sporting events from British Consular officials in Canada, West Germany, Portugal, Spain and the United States.

Some 90 letters were received from Members of the House of Commons and three from Members of the House of Lords. Some 1610 letters were received from the general public.

APPENDIX 2

SPORTS GROUNDS VISITED

Football

Arsenal
Blackburn Rovers
Blackpool
Chelsea
Liverpool
Manchester City
Manchester United
Middlesbrough
Millwall
Newcastle United
Preston North End
Sheffield Wednesday
Sunderland
Tottenham Hotspur

Glasgow Celtic
Glasgow Rangers
St Johnstone

International Stadia

Hampden Park
Wembley Stadium

Overseas Stadia

Stade des Costières, Nimes
Stadion Galgenwaard, Utrecht
Stadio Flaminio, Rome
Stadio Olimpico, Rome
Stadio San Siro, Milan

Cricket

The Oval

Golf

The Belfry, Sutton Coldfield

Lawn Tennis

Wimbledon

Rugby League

Salford

Rugby Union

Cardiff Arms Park
Murrayfield
Twickenham

REPORT OF THE TECHNICAL WORKING PARTY

22 December 1989

Dear Sir Peter

You invited the Technical Working Party "to review technical aspects of the guide to Safety at Sports Grounds; identify areas requiring clarification or amendment; and recommend accordingly." I have pleasure in submitting its Report, which has been agreed by all members. Detailed supplementary notes dealing with certain of the technical features will be available for your use in due course.

We note that the Guide is not confined to football grounds and stadia but includes guidance on all sports grounds, and we have borne this in mind in our considerations. Although not within our terms of reference, and for that reason not addressed in our Report, we recognise that efficient and effective stewarding is an integral element of crowd control and safety. Our recommendations complement, rather than supplant, the need for such stewarding.

The Technical Working Party met first on 18 October and held five formal day-long meetings supplemented by many working papers and informal discussions during the period available for report. The heavy pressures of the timetable could not have been accommodated without the fullest co-operation of those concerned, and I record my thanks to all members of the Technical Working Party and to its Secretary for the integrity, commitment and enthusiasm with which they approached the task.

LEONARD MAUNDER

REPORT OF THE TECHNICAL WORKING PARTY

The Green Guide

1. The Technical Working Party recognises the valuable contributions of successive editions of the Guide to Safety at Sports Grounds, commonly known as the Green Guide. Its scope and status are described in its introduction as follows: "This booklet provides guidance to ground management, local authorities and technical specialists such as engineers on measures for improving spectator safety at existing sports grounds. It is a voluntary guide and has no legal force".

2. In view of the variability of existing sports grounds in function and in scale, there are serious difficulties in establishing comprehensive and general regulations, backed by legal force, to cover all the complex details of design and construction. Adherence to the standards set by Building Regulations should provide a measure of uniformity in respect of new work at sports grounds. Nevertheless, the Technical Working Party is strongly of the opinion that a much higher degree of standardisation than presently prevails should be sought in practice.

3. It considers that a revised issue of the Green Guide should form the basis on which a designated ground or stand is certified by the certifying authority, and recommends that any departures from its guidance on technical provisions that may arise from local circumstances should be fully defined and should be subject to approval in writing by the certifying authority.

A Centre of Expertise

4. The Green Guide covers a wide range of material, much of which concerns the physical characteristics of grounds. Its successive issues have been published in response to a number of serious accidents at football grounds. This process has led to incremental advances in the Guide as experience has grown, but the Technical Working Party does not believe that such a process, although essential, is by itself sufficient to cope with present-day requirements.

5. Many British football grounds were first constructed a long time ago, and improvements have been introduced largely on an individual basis. A central body of knowledge applicable to the complex design of

such grounds has been conspicuously absent although a start has now been made. As a result, progress has been piecemeal.

6. The Technical Working Party considers that this is a serious defect. A continuous and expanding body of public knowledge, drawn from the relevant professional fields, is required to provide a basis for good individual designs at modern standards. At a time when substantial improvements are under consideration, including a higher proportion of seated accommodation, it is imperative to establish and to disseminate rigorous standards of design if expectations are to be fulfilled. The work of organisations in other countries, including the Comitato Olimpico Nazionale Italiano (CONI), can provide a valuable reference. The Technical Working Party recognises, too, the important work undertaken in this country by the Sports Council. Its recent guide to the planning, design and management of indoor arenas is a noteworthy attempt to draw together a considerable body of research and practical experience. Similarly, other work on outdoor stadia has taken place and is currently proceeding under the Council's aegis. It is important that resulting publications should be widely disseminated and that any guidance on outdoor stadia should make particular reference to the structural aspects of safety, comfort and crowd control.

7. The Technical Working Party therefore recommends the formation of a central body, under a title such as the Advisory Council for Sports Grounds, to provide an authoritative source of knowledge for all those involved in the design and construction of outdoor stadia. A detailed specification of its structure and funding is not proposed at this stage but, as envisaged, its members would be drawn from the relevant professional fields and would commission specialist advice when necessary. It would be independent of any Inspectorate. The relationship of such a body to other organisations is a matter for further discussion, but it is suggested that the Football Association and the Sports Council might wish to play leading roles.

Seating and Standing

8. The Technical Working Party notes that FIFA has agreed regulations on seating for certain classes of football matches, and that the regulations are to be imposed within a short time-scale. It also recognises that the British tradition of standing on terraces runs counter to these international requirements.

9. It is clear that if British clubs are to continue within the international community, they will be obliged to close their standing accommodation for matches that fall within the FIFA definition. For other matches, the Technical Working Party recognises that, whilst standing accommodation is not intrinsically unsafe, the benefits to spectator comfort and crowd control brought about by all-seater stadia are likely to accelerate the move towards such venues. The Technical Working Party accepts, however, that although the introduction of all-seater stadia for leading, well-supported football clubs may be both beneficial and practical, clubs in the lower divisions may find it less so and the removal of all standing accommodation at these grounds may affect their viability. Alterations to seating from standing arrangements at existing grounds may have both design and cost implications through the impact on such matters as spectator sight-lines and crowd density.

10. In addition, it must be recognised that there are many sports (horse, greyhound, motor racing and car rallying for example) where the nature of the sport favours the mobility of large sections of the crowd and where viewing from standing areas is an essential element. Any recommendations towards all-seater stadia must therefore be carefully worded.

Capacities

11. The Technical Working Party recognises that the safe allowable capacity of any viewing area, whether seated or standing, is the least of (i) its holding capacity, (ii) the number of persons who can leave through a normal exit system within a prescribed time at the end of an event, (iii) the number of persons who can leave through an emergency exit system within a prescribed time, and (iv) the number of persons who can be admitted through the turnstiles serving that area within one hour.

12. The theoretical holding capacity of a seated viewing area is simply the number of seats in good condition which comply with the relevant Green Guide recommendations including those relating to distance from exits and gangways and size and spacing. Determination of the holding capacity of a viewing terrace or slope is not so simple; factors that must be taken into account include the strength and spacing of the crush-barriers, the position of gangways, the dimensions and physical state of the steps, the effective standing area, and the acceptable packing density.

13. A packing density of $5.4/m^2$ is recommended in the current Green Guide as the maximum allowable figure for terraces and viewing slopes that meet all the specified guidelines. A reduced figure of $2.7/m^2$ is

presently recommended for areas deviating materially from the guidelines. The Technical Working Party sees no point in retaining reference to the lower figure and recommends that there should be no lower limit to the reduction; ie if the enclosure had such poor safety standards that it was totally unfit as a viewing area the figure should be zero.

14. As to the maximum figures, the Technical Working Party concludes that a uniformly distributed density of $5.4/m^2$ should be safe in static conditions where the terraces are in full compliance with the Green Guide. It recognises, however, that there will be variations of density within a given enclosure, and allowance should be made to accommodate this factor in the final determination.

15. The Technical Working Party recommends that the maximum allowable average packing density determined by the Inquiry should establish a general reference for certifying authorities. For an individual ground, the packing density applicable to a given standing area should be derived from this figure, the full figure for areas in good condition and reduced figures for areas in poorer condition. Detailed calculations of holding capacities should then be determined on the basis of the agreed packing density for that specific enclosure or other relevant factors. These calculations should take into account specific features of the crush-barriers and fences and of step dimensions as illustrated in the Green Guide. The Technical Working Party recommends a thorough review of the examples currently contained in Chapter 16 of the Green Guide, and the inclusion of appropriate diagrams.

Structural Elements

16. It is a fundamental requirement of safety that structures at grounds should provide spectators with safe accommodation and safe means of ingress and egress. They should also enable police and stewards to exert proper control over crowd movements. If a conflict should occur between these objectives, a substantial re-arrangement may be required; in no circumstances should safety standards be compromised. The Technical Working Party recommends that references to sub-divisions in Chapter 14 of the Green Guide be reviewed with these considerations in mind, and that the Chapter as a whole should reflect these principles more positively.

Separation of Viewing Areas and Pitch

17. The Technical Working Party recognises the importance of physical barriers as deterrents to pitch invasions. It also recognises that not all viewing areas present the same risk, and recommends that consideration be given to differentiating those areas requiring higher levels of security from other areas, such as seated accommodation and members' enclosures, where a lesser degree of security might be acceptable.

18. The general principle of separation endorsed by the Technical Working Party is that the means adopted should provide sufficient security against pitch incursions to enable the police to take timely and effective action should such incidents occur. Clearly a balance has to be struck between crowd control and safety.

19. A configuration recommended for wider consideration consists of a perimeter barrier on the pitch-side backed by a parallel and continuous crush-barrier on the terrace-side, set back from the perimeter barrier so as to provide a clear walk-way between the two; except in emergencies, spectators would not be allowed to enter the walk-way. Such an arrangement would reduce the risks associated with a common feature of British grounds, namely that the front steps of terraces are substantially lower than the level of the pitch: immediate attention should be given to the elimination of this hazard.

20. The Technical Working Party recommends that the maximum height of perimeter fences should be determined in relation to the UEFA standard of 2.2m. It also recommends the removal of overhanging sections and spiked or barbed-wire attachments at the tops of fences.

21. A form of separation increasingly adopted in new stadia is the dry moat. To be effective, a dry moat must be sufficiently wide and deep, and should be protected by fences on both sides to ensure that spectators and players do not fall into it. Where enough space is available, a moat may offer an attractive solution, but its application to older grounds is likely to be restricted by limitations of space.

Emergency Access to Pitch

22. The Technical Working Party recommends that emergency access to the pitch should be provided from all adjacent viewing areas. It considers the provision of gates or gaps in any formal barrier to be in all cases advantageous for the evacuation of adjacent enclosures and essential except where adequate, safe

alternative arrangements exist. Where fences, barriers or moats are installed the majority view of the Technical Working Party is that there should be clear gangways leading to emergency exits on to the pitch. Such gangways must be properly identified and kept clear at all times. The exit gates or gaps should be at least 1.1 metres wide or as wide as the gangways feeding into them, whichever is the larger and should be sufficient in dimensions and spacing to allow evacuation of the enclosure within a prescribed time. The Working Party recorded a minority view that the need to police gangways exacerbated friction on terraces, and that gangways were not always essential for proper crowd control and safety.

Crush Barriers

23. A review of the procedures for inspection and testing of barriers is recommended. The Technical Working Party considers that greater emphasis should be given to thorough recorded and certified annual visual inspections of all crush barriers. Particular attention should be given to the development of corrosion.

24. It is further recommended that 25% of barriers, evenly spaced through each enclosure as designated by a competent engineer, continue to be tested each year. In addition, all barriers which the inspection has identified as of possibly sub-standard condition should also be tested.

25. The adopted test method should be capable of applying to barrier rail, post and foundation anchorage, a loading equivalent to a uniformly distributed load 1.20 x the design load of the barrier as at present.

26. The test procedure should be revised in line with current practice for structural testing to incorporate (i) a detailed visual inspection of the barrier, (ii) a bedding-in cycle taken to a percentage of the design loading and (iii) a single cycle of proof testing taken as at present to 1.20 x the design loading. Deflections at all significant points should be recorded.

27. After the full proof load has been held for a minimum of five minutes the deflections should be recorded prior to release of loading and the permanent residual unloaded deflections recorded after the load has been released.

28. The Technical Working Party recommends the adoption of two criteria for acceptable structural performance (i) that no significant defects, including corrosion, are revealed by inspection and (ii) that the percentage recovery of deflections after release of the load during proof-testing achieves acceptable values. The specific values required will depend on the materials of construction.

29. The Technical Working Party recommends that the distinction currently drawn in the Green Guide between "peak" and "non-peak" viewing areas for the purpose of assessing barrier spacing should be abolished. All areas should comply with the peak viewing specifications.

Stands

30. A substantial part of Chapter 10 of the Green Guide, 'Roofed Stands with Seated Accommodation', deals with temporary structures. It is recommended that this material should be placed in a separate Chapter, and that it should give explicit references as required to British Standards and to applicable regulations.

31. The remainder, which might be called 'Covered Standing and Seated Accommodation', should clarify the special requirements for safety that are involved, noting that fire risk is not the only hazard and that statutory control of the requirements may be vested in different authorities. Appropriate references to Building Regulations should be made. It is important to ensure that all spectators can be cleared into safe protected escape routes within prescribed times, although such routes need not be exits from the stand as a whole.

Ingress/Egress

32. The current Chapters on Ingress and Egress in the Green Guide (Chapters 5 and 6) contain much useful information, but are nonetheless in need of some revision. Consideration was given by the Technical Working Party to the possible amalgamation of features common to both ingress and egress, but despite the common ground it is recognised that emphases might well differ. The Working Party does not therefore recommend amalgamation of the individual Chapters.

Ingress

33. The Technical Working Party felt that Chapter 5 needed expansion to incorporate additional clauses on (a) the positive counting and recording of those passing through each turnstile; (b) the location of

amenities inside the ground to avoid obstructing or disrupting the flow between turnstile and enclosures; (c) the sub-division of enclosures; (d) the adequacy of well distributed entrances into large enclosures to facilitate even packing; and (e) the design of entrances so as to avoid local pressure on spectators caused, for example, by downward ramps. Informative diagrams should be adopted and general principles laid down, wherever possible. The Technical Working Party would not favour the introduction of numerical examples which might, in any event, be difficult to establish. It views the current maximum notional flow rate per turnstile of 750 persons per hour (as set out in paragraph 47 Green Guide) as too high, and recommends a figure of 500 as the median for a normal turnstile. Furthermore, it recommends that variations up or down be approved by the certifying authority, subject to a maximum upper limit of 660 persons per hour.

Egress

34. Greater cross-referencing with other Chapters is required, and the Technical Working Party favours expansion or amendment of a number of paragraphs. In particular, the density figure set out in paragraph 54 in respect of reservoir areas is felt to be too high, and the members of the Technical Working Party recommend that, where reservoir areas cannot be removed from egress routes, a lower density of 35-40 persons per 10 sq metres be substituted. The Technical Working Party favours greater emphasis on networking, and believes that the Green Guide should include a stipulation that each ground produce proper, networked plans, delineating all aspects of ingress/egress.

Enclosures/Turnstiles

35. The Technical Working Party strongly recommends that there should be a direct one-to-one relationship between banks of turnstiles and enclosures in order to maintain accurate counts of entries. A review of the current state of League grounds had shown that sub-divisions such as had occurred at Hillsborough were uncommon, and had generally been initiated by police for crowd control. Where such sub-divisions do exist, it is imperative that the total number of spectators entering each sub-division should be counted separately.

Stairways and Ramps

36. The Technical Working Party notes the dangers presented by stairways and ramps, particularly those used by the public in large numbers, and recommends extensive redrafting of the Green Guide to present more sharply the hazards involved. It recognises that the standards of safety required for stairways and ramps which form part of the access between enclosures and an exit and those which exist as gangways within enclosures differ and recommends that the differences be explained in more detail. Particular attention should be given by certifying authorities to acceptable upper limits on the gradients of ramps and stairways. The maximum gradient for ramps set out in the current Green Guide was felt acceptable.

37. Similarly, the Working Party believes that the channelling of flows by the provision of handrails should be given greater emphasis. The recommended width of channel for both stairways and ramps should not exceed three persons (unit widths) in line abreast, and the width of up to 1.8 metres permitted by paragraph 76 should therefore be reduced accordingly. Handrails should extend, by at least 300mm beyond the top and bottom of any stairway or ramp.

38. The difference between handrails, balustrades and barriers on or near the top and bottom of stairways and ramps, and their appropriate strength requirements, needs to be clarified.

39. The Technical Working Party recommends the inclusion in the Green Guide of a greater number of diagrams illustrating the potentially hazardous situations in relation to stairways and ramps and of the principles behind the provisions.

Inspections and Tests

40. Inspection and tests of all equipment and structures at grounds are vital features of good operation. Their range is wide, extending from visual inspection before and after each event to regular testing of structural components. It is a matter of serious concern that the interpretation of requirements by those responsible is unacceptably variable. The Technical Working Party considers that action should be taken to ensure that common high standards of inspection and test are realised, and makes the following recommendations.

(i) The Green Guide should include a comprehensive tabulation of inspections and tests covering the essential technical features of grounds. It should prescribe the minimum frequencies at which the inspections and tests should be conducted.

(ii) The required levels of competence of those carrying out the inspections and tests should be defined.

(iii) Records of the results of inspections and tests, including the identification of defects and the remedies adopted, should be certified by those carrying out the work.

(iv) A national Inspectorate should be established to oversee the adoption of common standards of inspection and test. Its terms of reference should include the compilation and maintenance of a national register of organisations employed to carry out inspections and tests; central recording of the extent and type of the inspections and tests adopted at individual grounds; and the provision of advice on inspection and test for those responsible for carrying out the work and for certifying authorities. It would be in the interest of common standards if an Inspectorate of this kind dealt with the grounds of all relevant sports, and consideration should be given to its formation through an association of their governing bodies.

Fire Safety

41. There is general recognition amongst Technical Working Party members that the current Chapter on Fire Safety (Chapter 11) is well-defined. It contains much useful advice on egress and means of escape, application of which is not restricted to fire risks and which would bear repetition in other Chapters.

42. The Technical Working Party considers that it is essential to maintain simple, clear lines of authority and communication; independent input from individual bodies is to be avoided. With that in mind, its members believe that consultation on all safety matters should be directly with the certifying authority who, in turn, would consult with the fire, police, and other authorities.

Emergency/Auxiliary Power

43. The Technical Working Party considers that the current Green Guide contains insufficient information on auxiliary power. It recommends a separate chapter on the topic with a requirement that emergency power should be sufficient to maintain an adequate level of lighting, and public address system and to operate any electronic gates, alarms etc for a period of three hours from the time of failure of the normal supply.

Communications

44. The Technical Working Party considers that too little weight has in the past been attached to the need for a comprehensive communications system, capable of reaching both inside and outside the ground.

45. Chapter 12 of the Green Guide therefore requires substantial amendment to reflect the importance of effective communications systems, the need to make use of high-technology equipment, and the value of closer co-operation between club and police personnel. The Technical Working Party considers that Interim Recommendations 31-34 should be retained permanently and incorporated into the Green Guide.

Disabled Spectators

46. The current Green Guide fails to address the specific problems encountered by disabled spectators and the Technical Working Party recommends the introduction of a Chapter to cover these aspects. It should deal in particular with Ingress and Egress and with the provision of self-contained viewing areas.

SUMMARY OF MAIN RECOMMENDATIONS

The Green Guide

1. A higher degree of standardisation in stadia design and construction is required. An updated and revised Green Guide should form the basis on which a designated ground or stand is certified. It should incorporate appropriate diagrams and refer to relevant Building Regulations.

Advisory Body

2. There should be a single, central body (called perhaps the Advisory Council for Sports Grounds) to provide an authoritative source of knowledge for all those involved in the design and construction of stadia.

Seating/Standing

3. Whilst standing accommodation is not intrinsically unsafe, all-seater stadia bring benefits to spectator comfort, safety and crowd control. The implementation of higher proportions of seated accommodation should be governed by common high standards of design and construction.

Capacities

4. Capacity depends on standards of ingress, egress and safety generally as well as the acceptable packing density and the effective area of the accommodation. The current maximum packing density of $5.4/m^2$ recommended in the Green Guide for standing terraces should be safe in static conditions where the terraces are in full compliance with the Green Guide. It should be recognised, however, that densities normally vary over an enclosure, and an allowable average figure should reflect this consideration. The reduced figure of $2.7/m^2$ should be abolished and there should be no specified lower limit. If an enclosure has such poor safety standards that it is totally unfit as a viewing area, the figure should be zero.

Separation of Viewing Areas and Pitch

5. Consideration should be given to different perimeter arrangements appropriate for different areas of a ground.

6. The means of separation adopted should provide sufficient protection against pitch incursions without compromising spectator safety. The maximum height of fences should be determined in relation to the UEFA standard of 2.2 metres. Overhanging sections and spiked or barbed-wire attachments should be removed.

7. Attention should be given to the elimination of spectator viewing from front steps of terraces which are substantially lower than the level of the pitch.

Emergency Access to the Pitch

8. Emergency access to the pitch should be provided from all adjacent viewing areas.

9. Exit gaps or gates should be at least 1.1 metres wide or as wide as the gangways feeding into them, whichever is the larger. All gangways must be clearly identified and must be kept clear of spectators in normal circumstances.

Crush Barriers

10. A review of the procedures for inspection and testing of barriers is recommended. Greater emphasis should be given to thorough recorded and certified annual visual inspections of all crush barriers, and to the establishment of an unambiguous testing procedure.

Stands

11. The Green Guide should contain a separate Chapter on temporary structures, with appropriate references to applicable regulations and British Standards.

Ingress

12. The current maximum notional flow rate per turnstile of 750 persons per hour is too high. A figure of 500 should be adopted as the median with a maximum upper limit of 660 persons per hour. Variations from the median must be approved by the certifying authority.

Egress

13. Where reservoir areas cannot be removed, a lower density of 35-40 persons per 10 sq metres should be adopted. Each ground should produce networked plans delineating all aspects of ingress and egress.

Enclosures/Turnstiles

14. There should be a direct one-to-one relationship between banks of turnstiles and corresponding enclosures. Where sub-divisions exist, it is imperative that the totals entering each sub-division are counted separately.

Stairways and Ramps

15. The recommended width of channels should not exceed three persons (unit widths) in line abreast. Handrails should extend by at least 300mm beyond the top and bottom of any stairway or ramp. The design and strength of handrails, barriers and protection on or near stairways or ramps should be clearly defined. Ramps should not produce dangerous crowd pressures.

Inspection and Tests

16. Action should be taken to ensure that common high standards of inspection and test are realised. A national Inspectorate should be established to oversee the adoption of such standards. Its terms of reference should include compilation and maintenance of a national register of organisations employed to carry out inspections and tests; central recording of the extent and type of inspections and tests at individual grounds; and the provision of advice.

Communications

17. The Green Guide should be amended substantially to emphasise the importance of effective communications systems capable of reaching both inside and outside the ground.

Disabled Spectators

18. The Green Guide should contain a separate Chapter to cover this subject.

MEMBERSHIP OF THE TECHNICAL WORKING PARTY

Professor Leonard Maunder, OBE, BSc, PhD, ScD, FEng, FIMechE (Chairman)
Assessor to the Hillsborough Stadium Disaster Inquiry

Mr L N Bush FRICS, CEng, MIStructE, FIAS
City Building Surveyor, City of Liverpool

Mr W H Carter MSST
George Corderoy & Co, Quantity Surveyors
(Nominated by the Football Association)

Mr M G T Dickson BA, MS, CEng, MIStructE
Buro Happold Consulting Engineers
(Nominated by the Institution of Structural Engineers)

Dr C E Nicholson PhD, CEng, MIM
Deputy Director, Research & Laboratory Services Division
Health and Safety Executive

Mr B A Stickley CEng, FIStructE
Directorate of Works, Home Office

Mr J C Sweet (Secretary)
Hillsborough Stadium Disaster Inquiry

FINAL REPORT OF MR JUSTICE POPPLEWELL'S INQUIRY

CHAPTER 2: HISTORY OF PREVIOUS INQUIRIES

2.1 When my Interim Report was published, it might have been thought by some that the suggestions which I set out had only recently been considered. It was said to be unfair to expect the football clubs to have taken earlier steps to arrange their affairs. It was urged that they should now be entitled to more time and more money in order to deal with the problems of crowd control and safety at their grounds. The problem of crowd control and safety had, so it was said, suddenly arisen. I have to say that almost all the matters into which I have been asked to inquire and almost all the solutions I have proposed have been previously considered in detail by many distinguished Inquiries over a period of sixty years.

The Shortt Report

2.2 On 11 June 1923, the then Secretary of State for the Home Department asked the Rt Hon Edward Shortt KC to form a Committee to inquire, amongst other things, into arrangements made to deal with the abnormally large attendances on special occasions, especially attendances at athletic grounds. This arose from disorder which occurred at Wembley Stadium on the occasion of the first Cup Final on 28 April 1923. The Committee reported on 13 March 1924. The Report was presented to Parliament and published as Command Paper 2088 at the princely sum of 6d.

2.3 About responsibility for control inside grounds the Report had this to say:

"As regards the general question of the apportionment of responsibility inside the ground as between the police and the ground authority, the principle to be followed should, in our judgment, be that the police should be responsible for all matters appertaining to the preservation of law and order and that for arrangements for the convenience of the public the ground authority should be responsible. It is, however, most important not only that the police arrangements should be under the control of a single officer, but also that the duties for which the ground authority is responsible should be assigned to a definite individual, who should be competent to give instructions and to deal with any incident which arises. If responsibility is definitely allocated in this matter it appears to us that, in ordinary circumstances, there need be no difficulty in this division of duties and that no disadvantage need result from the existence of dual control so long as the closest co-operation is maintained between the two authorities at all times. We are of the opinion, however, that if any emergency arises or there appears to be the slightest probability of a disturbance, it is essential that control should pass into the hands of one individual, and we recommend that, in the case of grounds providing accommodation for more than 10,000 persons, on all occasions when specially large attendances are anticipated or for other reasons unusual excitement is to be expected, arrangements should be concerted beforehand by which one individual can at any moment take control of the situation."

2.4. That paragraph of the report continued:

"The question in such circumstances would have become one of the preservation of law and order and we therefore have no doubt that the control should then pass into the hands of the senior police officer present, and we consider that such officer would be justified in any circumstances, whether in accordance with a pre-arranged scheme or not, in assuming control if he considered it necessary for the purpose of the restoration of order. As part of the arrangements for this purpose we think that, in the very large grounds, there should be a central control box in telephonic communication with all parts of the ground and that the principal police and ground officials should be stationed there so that they may be in constant touch with the situation."...(Paragraph22).

2.5 About stewards the Report said:

"We understand that there is no uniform practice with regard to the employment of stewards at sports grounds, that in some cases they are only used to show spectators into the seating accommodation, and that, in cases where stewards are employed for packing of the standing room, they are only employed when there are specially large crowds. We consider it desirable in the interests of safety that, for the purpose of handling a crowd, stewards should be employed in any case where the crowd is likely to approach the capacity of the ground. For seating accommodation stewards should always be employed. It is in the highest degree important that any such stewards should be properly trained in their work and intimately acquainted with the

part of the ground placed under their charge. We doubt whether it is practicable to secure suitable men for this purpose unless they are given continual experience in the work, and we therefore recommend that every ground with a capacity exceeding 10,000 which provides terraced accommodation for its spectators should maintain, or have a call upon, an adequate staff of efficient stewards, and should ensure that they keep proficient by requiring them to perform duty at frequent intervals. Stewards should be organised as a disciplined body and should act under the control and supervision of their own officers. They should wear a distinctive badge of authority, which they should not be able easily to discard." (Paragraph 27).

2.6 The Report had this to say about precautions against fire:

"We have been somewhat surprised to find that in many cases little or not precaution is taken against the risk of fire in stands. We do not suppose that either the risk or the consequences of fire would be so serious in an open stand as in a closed building, but we consider it most important that adequate arrangements should be made to deal with any outbreak which might occur." (Paragraph 40).

but concluded generally:

"We are assured that these governing bodies are only too anxious to secure that their sport is carried on under conditions which will promote the public safety, and we feel that at this stage it is safe to leave the matter to them." (Paragraph 47).

The Moelwyn Hughes Report

2.7 The next report (published as Cmnd 6846) arose out of the disaster at Bolton Wanderers' Football Ground on 9 March 1946. Mr R Moelwyn Hughes KC was appointed by the then Home Secretary to conduct an enquiry into the circumstances of the disaster which arose by the presence of some 85,000 spectators. 50,000 had been expected. Because of the press of people in an enclosure two barriers collapsed and 33 people were killed.

2.8 It is interesting to observe that the previous best attendance at Bolton in the 1945-46 season had been 43,000 and it was amply policed by a force of 60. On this occasion there were 103 police to control 85,000 spectators, which is about 1/10th of the present ratio of police to spectators at football grounds both inside and outside the ground.

2.9 Mr Hughes made a number of recommendations. He said:

"Burnden Park is typical of most home grounds of the leading football teams in the country. They have grown stage by stage from humble beginnings on sites acquired when the large gates of these days were not anticipated, or when the clubs had not achieved eminence. It would be idle to suggest that the grounds, or large sections of them, should be rebuilt, but if they are to be made reasonably safe and if the risk of repeating the tragedy of Burnden Park is to be avoided, then, I have formed the clear view that the following steps must be taken . . ." (Page 10).

2.10 The recommendations included inspections of the enclosures, scientific calculation of the maximum number to be allowed entry, counting those entering the ground by mechanical means and central co-ordination of the system, all to ensure the admission of a safe number of spectators.

2.11 So far as future regulation was concerned the Report said:

"The preceding safety measures cannot be secured without legislation. A Departmental Committee reporting on Crowds to a previous Home Secretary in 1924 (Cd 2088) anaemically recommended that adequate provision for safety be left to the pressure of the governing bodies in sport. The most important of these was, of course, the Football Association, which had not deigned to appear before the Committee . . .

The legislation should empower the Home Secretary to issue general regulations for different kinds of grounds and the broad conditions necessary for safety.

No ground of any considerable size should be opened to the public until it has been licenced by, I suggest as an appropriate licensing authority, the local authority. The issue of the licence would depend upon satisfying the authority as to the construction and equipment of the ground, its compliance with regulations and the proposed maximum figures of admission to the different parts."

2.12 Mr Hughes went on to say:

"Compliance with the recommendations of this Report will cost money. They will involve grounds in a loss of gate money on popular days . . . The insurance for greater safety for the public demands a premium."

Mr Hughes ended his report by saying:

"I earnestly hope that, if the proposals I have made in this Report, or similar suggestions, commend themselves to you, Parliament will not be slow in granting you the necessary powers." (Pages 11-12).

The Chester Report

2.13 Mr Hughes' words fell on deaf ears. It was another 22 years before there was a further report commissioned by the Government on the problems of football. In June 1966, the then Secretary of State for Education and Science appointed Mr Norman Chester CBE, as he then was (Warden of Nuffield College, Oxford), to chair an Enquiry. His terms of reference were:

"To enquire into the state of Association Football at all levels, including the organisation, management, finance and administration, and the means by which the game may be developed for the public good; and to make recommendations."

2.14 Mr Chester made this observation about crowd behaviour:

"In recent years there has been an increase in disorderly behaviour by spectators. During the period 1946-1960 there were 195 cases brought to the attention of the FA, an average of 13 per season. In the following six seasons 148 cases were reported, an average of 25 per season. The matter was discussed some time ago at a meeting between representatives of a number of police forces (including the British Transport Police), the Football Association and the Football League. Both these governing bodies have been very concerned at this development."

2.15 The Report continued:

"We have not been able to devote the time and resources to the study of this problem which its complexity deserves. We very much welcome the initiative of the Birmingham Research Group, of which Dr J A Harrington is Research Director and have been fortunate enough to see the Group's preliminary report. We are sure that its findings will be of value to all concerned." (Page 97).

The Harrington Report

2.16 This was made to the then Minister of Sport.[1] It observed:

"Some spectators carry knives, hammers, sticks and spikes, choppers, and other offensive weapons like powdered pepper which are not necessarily used for violent purposes but may be used in threatening displays. There is also the problem of singing or chanting bawdy or obscene songs and phrases some of which are also threatening and provocative." (Page 8).

2.17 About riots the Report said:

"While such riots must be regarded as almost unknown accompaniments of football in this country, their potential seriousness and danger were exemplified recently by football riots in Turkey, where many people were reported killed. While comparable riots seem unlikely here, it would be foolish to rule out the possibility of much more serious crowd disturbances at football matches than we have yet experienced." (Page 9).

2.18 The Report regretted inactivity thus far:

"The question of public safety and crowd control at football matches was dealt with by a departmental committee report published in 1924 (Cond. 2088) and the inquiry into the disaster at the Bolton Wanderers Football Ground in 1946 (Cond. 6946) . . . Unfortunately the most helpful suggestions in these reports have often been ignored, though the committee's recommendations do carry some weight with boards of football clubs".

2.19 The Report went on:

"The absence of national legislation outlining minimum standards of safety and amenity at football grounds means that some club managements do not feel obliged to put their grounds into a state considered by the police to be necessary for crowd control." (Page 33).

---

[1] "Soccer Hooliganism: A preliminary Report." Bristol: John Wright and Sons Ltd 1968.

2.20 And continued:

"We feel that improved ground facilities would not only help to deal with the hooligan problem but do something towards its prevention. Clubs often seem keener to spend money on the purchase of players than to undertake any major spending on ground improvement which would increase safety and make hooligan control easier. The loss of revenue which a club may suffer from alterations may be the determining factor. There is of course no obligation on a club to convert a ground which can accommodate 50,000 to one which takes a smaller number in conditions of greater safety and comfort. Letters from members of the public suggest that already some are staying away because of their dislike of poor facilities, overcrowding, and disturbances, so that the neglect of ground improvement may ultimately be self defeating." (Page 34).

2.21 So far as responsibility is concerned, the Report said:

"We think that those responsible for club management and the governing bodies of football should accept far more responsibility for keeping their crowds in order. This applies not only within the stadium itself but to club supporters travelling in groups to and from matches. One gets the impression that some clubs disclaim any responsibility for the behaviour of their supporters and if the atmosphere of a Roman holiday is not deliberately fostered it is looked on with considerable tolerance. Football matches are commercial enterprises conducted for profit on private premises and clubs have therefore a heavy responsibility for keeping order and safety for the public on their premises." (Pages 35-36).

2.22 In its summary the Report concluded:

"The solution of the problem of hooliganism in the football stadium is ultimately the responsibility of individual clubs who must each deal with it in the light of local circumstances. While a few clubs are exemplary in their attitude to the problem others are *laissez-faire* and need persuasion to take a more active role in trying to control hooliganism in their own grounds. This *laissez-faire* attitude does not help the police in their attempts to deal with the matter." (Page 56).

The Lang Report

2.23 Shortly thereafter, a Working Party under the chairmanship of Sir John Lang GCB and including a number of distinguished members, was appointed by the then Minister with special responsibility for Sport to examine the problems involved in football crowd behaviour to which attention had been called a few months previously by the Harrington Report. Sir John's Report was presented on 21 November 1969.

2.24 By way of introduction it said:

"The Working Party was dealing with a subject which has been discussed almost *ad nauseam* during recent years. Not unexpectedly the Working Party has not found a single simple solution for a problem which is often due to a combination of factors . . ." (Page 3).

2.25 The members of the Inquiry witnessed the demonstration of CCTV equipment and reported:

". . . the view was formed that closed circuit television could be of value in the general subject of crowd control and . . . would be an important factor in preventing misbehaviour by spectators at grounds. It was a refinement which most of the top class clubs could be expected eventually to have as a matter of course." (Page 9).

2.26 About alcohol the Report said:

"There can be no doubt that consumption of alcohol is an important factor in crowd misbehaviour, both because it stimulates quarrelsomeness and because empty bottles are dangerous missiles. There would be no advantage in refusing licence facilities to football club grounds - this would merely stimulate spectators to bring their supplies from outside." (Page 14).

The Wheatley Report

2.27 On 4 February 1971 the Rt Hon Lord Wheatley was asked by the then Secretary of State for the Home Department and the then Secretary of State for Scotland to make an independent appraisal of the effectiveness of existing arrangements for crowd safety at sports grounds in Great Britain, and of the improvements which could be brought about within the present framework of the law, and to consider the nature of any alterations in the law which appeared to be needed. This arose from the disaster at Ibrox Park where 66 spectators died.

2.28 On 16 March 1972 Lord Wheatley completed his Report and it was presented to Parliament and published by HMSO as Cmnd. 4952.

2.29 The Report contained a technical Appendix. Following the Report, the Safety of Sports Grounds Act 1975 was passed. A licensing system involving the issue of a safety certificate for designated grounds was introduced and supporting guidance (the Green Guide) was published. In his Report Lord Wheatley said:

"I recognise that a decision to introduce a licensing system for grounds along the lines I have recommended may cause anxiety to some football clubs and football administrators. As I see it, their misgivings are associated with a fear that such stringent conditions might be attached to the granting of a licence that many clubs may not be able to afford the cost and some may have to go out of business." (Paragraph 66).

2.30 **"My answer to that is this. My task was to consider the problem of crowd safety at the grounds. Clubs which charge the public for admission have a duty to see that their grounds are reasonably safe for spectators. That is a primary consideration. It is accordingly necessary that some standards should be imposed and observed. This has been recognised by the football authorities themselves ... I have canvassed all the alternatives that have been proposed or which I personally thought were reasonable to consider, and the one which I decided was best to meet the situation in the interest of the public is the licensing system by a local authority. There is nothing new in this proposal. It has been mooted for almost fifty years. It can come as no surprise to the football world, and in the light of happenings over the years the demand for an independent appraisal and determination of the safety of grounds becomes almost irresistible. I certainly cannot resist it."** (Paragraph 67).

2.31 Lord Wheatley ended his Report by saying:

"I trust that this Report may be of assistance to you in deciding what should be done to solve this important question of crowd safety in football grounds. One thing is certain. The public demand for something to be done has been growing over the years. I am sure I am reflecting public opinion when I say that something must be done now. The evidence certainly supports that view."

The McElhone Report

2.32 In October 1976 the then Secretary of State for Scotland asked Mr Frank McElhone MP to chair a Working Group on Football Crowd Behaviour.

"to consider the problems caused by some Scottish football supporters and to make recommendations to the Scottish Football Association and other organisations concerned."

Among the membership of the Working Group were representatives from the football authorities, from the football clubs and the Strathclyde Police.

2.33 In the introduction to the Report[2], Mr McElhone said:

"There is no simple solution to the problem; it is but one of the manifestations of anti-social behaviour besetting society in general today. We have however in our findings arrived at a number of conclusions and recommendations which we hope, given a commitment to implement them on the part of all those most closely concerned, will go some way towards reducing the problem of hooliganism at football matches and by so doing turn football grounds once again into places of entertainment where parents can take their children to enjoy, in relative comfort and safety, the pleasures of our national game."

2.34 The Report observed that:

"A hooligan is a hooligan no matter where he operates and the fact that his behaviour is conspicuous at a football match has very often nothing to do with the game itself." (Paragraph 4).

Mr McElhone saw the problem as one of trying to reduce, or at least contain, the incidence of hooliganism at football matches without restricting the pleasure of the majority of supporters.

---

[2]Report of the Working Group on Football Crowd Behaviour: Scottish Education Department/HMSO 1977.

2.35 So far as drink was concerned, the Report recommended that it should be an offence for a spectator to carry or attempt to carry alcohol into a football ground; that is should be an offence to be in possession of alcohol within the ground or to attempt to gain admission while drunk. The Report recommended that more people who were physically capable of carrying out the duties of enforcement would have to be recruited and suggested that, in their recruitment of stewards, clubs should look to their supporters' clubs to assist in providing the kind of men required for the job. So far as transport was concerned, the Report recommended that it should be an offence for anyone to be in possession of alcoholic liquor on a vehicle hired specifically for the purpose of carrying passengers bound for a football match; or to allow any alcoholic liquor to be carried on a public service vehicle being used for the purpose of carrying passengers to football matches; or to allow the carriage of any drunken person on such a vehicle bound for a football match.

2.36 So far as the separation of supporters was concerned the Report recommended:

"That in the interests of crowd control and safety, separation of rival supporters at turnstiles should be carried out if the police, in consultation with the club, consider such a step to be necessary; that for matches where larger than average attendances are expected, sufficient turnstiles should be opened timeously in order to achieve speedy admission." (Recommendation 13).

"In order to protect players, match officials and the pitch, access to the playing area should be made as difficult as possible. To prevent an invasion of the playing area by spectators ... the erection of a physical barrier in the form of a fence not less than 1.8 metres in height with access points to allow the pitch to be used if necessary for the evacuation of spectators in an emergency." (Paragraph 53).

2.37 A further recommendation was that:

"the Courts should make full use of the higher fining powers under the Criminal Law Act 1977 in respect of common law offences which include malicious mischief, breach of the peace and assault, these being the most common offences associated with football hooliganism, and in respect of persistent offenders, should normally impose imprisonment without option." (Recommendation 19).

2.38 The Report recommended that:

"The police should have statutory powers to search for any containers ... in the possession of any person entering or attempting to enter football grounds." (Recommendation 24).

but went on to point out that the clubs must bear their share of the responsibility for the behaviour and conduct of their staff at all levels:

2.39 Among other observations the Report says this:

"We recognise that many football grounds in Scotland are very old; some could even be described as primitive in that not only do they lack any kind of comfort for spectators but they also lack basic amenities including adequate toilet accommodation. This primitive environment encourages some people to react in a primitive manner. Moreover there is a strong case for more seating accommodation. In our view it would go a considerable way towards reducing hooliganism; potential trouble spots could be more quickly recognised and identification of troublemakers by police would be made that much easier."

The Report therefore recommended:

"that clubs should consider the provision of additional seating accommodation. In addition clubs must provide adequate toilet facilities for men *and* women and generally improve amenities for spectators." (Paragraph 88).

2.40 This Report also recommended that:

"players should be encouraged by the clubs to extend their voluntary public relations work in the community including personal appearances at youth clubs etc and coaching sessions in schools with the objects of promoting the game and the concept of good sportsmanship." (Recommendation 37).

CCTV was recommended and supporters' clubs encouraged. The Scottish Football Association was recommended to take appropriately firm action against clubs.

Department of the Environment Working Group

2.41 The most recent Government publication on the subject of football is the Report of an Official Working Group on Football Spectator Violence set up by Department of the Environment, which was published by HMSO in 1984. The Working Group was set up following incidents of violence involving British supporters at England's soccer matches in Luxembourg and France in November 1983 and February 1984 respectively. It dealt party with problems arising out of international football.

2.42 However, as regards domestic football the Report said:

"the Group reaffirmed the importance of consistent planning, preparation and co-ordination; of building on experience; and of the need to consider afresh all possible measures, including those previously thought to be impractical or unnecessary." (Paragraph 5.1).

"We recommend therefore that the FA reviews and better defines its powers and procedures and the responsibilities of the clubs. If their powers prove to be inadequate, the Association should consider enhancing them."

The Report went on:

"This would better equip the FA to implement some of the recommendations." (Paragraph 5.5).

2.43 The Football Association had issued a "blueprint" detailing the precautions which league clubs should take against violence, which was circulated to clubs at the beginning of the 1983-84 season. The Working Party Report said that it:

"... has not been rigorously adopted by all clubs. Since it represents the collective wisdom of football clubs, many of whom have successfully countered serious threats of violence, its implementation should have prevented some of the violence in grounds last season." (Paragraph 5.7).

2.44 The Report observed that the enforcement by the Football Association of its "blueprint" occurs after the event when the deficiencies in a club's planning has become apparent. The Report recommended that:

"improved means should be found for ensuring that clubs adopt the provisions of the "blueprint" in a way appropriate to their own grounds and matches." (Paragraph 5.7).

The Report went on to recommend that each club should produce a detailed set of plans to be submitted to the football authorities for endorsement. This would prevent some clubs from avoiding their responsibilities and might ensure also a more co-operative and committed response.

2.45 The Report recommended that matches between high risk clubs should be programmed so that the risk or threat of violence could be reduced. The Report said:

"It is more likely to take place at the beginning and end of the season and at holiday periods, particularly at seaside fixtures when other groups of young people sometimes also clash with football supporters." (Paragraph 5.13).

2.46 The Report went on to recommend the introduction of club membership, the introduction of CCTV and closer links with the community. It did not recommend that alcohol should be banned in grounds and concluded that in the absence of clear evidence that the introduction of legislation along the lines of the Criminal Justice (Scotland) Act 1980 would reduce violence at English soccer matches, it could not recommend such action. Furthermore, said the Report:

"legislation of this kind would be unwelcome to many; the majority of football clubs are untroubled by violence and would unnecessarily be penalised financially and the vast majority of non-violent spectators would suffer for the actions of the few." (Paragraph 5.34):

The Working Group did not recommend additional measures for banning alcohol on trains or on football coaches.

Conclusion

2.47 A study of all these reports (and there are numerous reports and discussion papers by other bodies) shows that the following are measures which have been frequently recommended:

1. Closed Circuit Television
2. Membership Cards
3. Segregation
4. More seating at football grounds
5. Encouragement of supporters' clubs
6. A ban on alcohol
7. Involvement of the clubs with the community
8. Heavier penalties

I too shall argue for these and related measures. It is to be hoped they will be more vigorously pursued by the appropriate bodies than in the past.

Appendix 5:   Stadion Galgenwaard, Utrecht.

Appendix 6:   **Perimeter fences at Liverpool (Anfield)**

Appendix 6:   Perimeter fences at Everton (Goodison Park)

107

Appendix 7:   The moat at Utrecht.

Appendix 8:   **The perimeter gates at Nimes (Stade des Costières).**

Printed in the United Kingdom for The Stationery Office Limited

Dd 5068048   5/98   3401   3840   Job No. J46635